THE HEIRS OF THE PROPHETS

THE HEIRS OF THE PROPHETS

Warathatu'l-Anbiyā'

IBN RAJAB AL-ḤANBALĪ

INTRODUCTION AND TRANSLATION BY

ZAID SHAKIR

THE STARLATCH PRESS

CHICAGO

Printed in the United States of America.

10 09 08 07 06 05 04 03 02 01   10 9 8 7 6 5 4 3 2 1

ISBN: 1-929694-12-1 (Sewn Softcover)

The Starlatch Press
phone/fax: (312) 896-7403
www.starlatch.com / info@starlatch.com

Design by ALW

This book is printed on premium acid-free paper that meets the minimum requirements set for alkaline papers by the American National Standard for Information Sciences—Permanence of paper for printed Library Materials, ANSI Z 39.48-1984.

Special thanks to Adnan Arain and Deanna Othman
for their work on the book.

For Shaykh Muṣṭafā al-Turkmānī

TRANSLITERATION KEY

ء	’ [1]	ر	r[6]	ف	f
ا	ā, a	ز	z	ق	q[13]
ب	b	س	s	ك	k
ت	t	ش	sh	ل	l
ث	th[2]	ص	ṣ[7]	م	m
ج	j	ض	ḍ[8]	ن	n
ح	ḥ[3]	ط	ṭ[9]	ه	h[14]
خ	kh[4]	ظ	ẓ[10]	و	ū, u, w
د	d	ع	ʿ [11]	ي	ī, i, y
ذ	dh[5]	غ	gh[12]		

ﷺ—Mentioned after the Prophet Muḥammad’s ﷺ name and translated as “may Allah bless him and grant him peace.”

﵇—Mentioned after the names of the prophets and translated as “peace be upon him.”

ؓ—Mentioned after the names of the Companions and righteous scholars and translated as “may Allah be pleased with him.”

---

1. A distinctive glottal stop made at the bottom of the throat. It is also used to indicate the running of two words into one, e.g., *bismi’Llāh*.
2. Should be pronounced like the *th* in think.
3. A hard *h* sound made at the Adam’s apple in the middle of the throat.
4. Pronounced like the *ch* in Scottish loch.
5. Should be pronounced like the *th* in this.
6. A slightly trilled *r* made behind the front teeth which is trilled not more than once or twice.
7. An emphatic *s* pronounced behind the upper front teeth.
8. An emphatic *d*-like sound made by pressing the entire tongue against the upper palate.
9. An emphatic *t* sound produced behind the front teeth.
10. An emphatic *th* sound, like the *th* in this, made behind the front teeth.
11. A distinctive Semitic sound made in the middle throat and sounding to a Western ear more like a vowel than a consonant.
12. A guttural sound made at the top of the throat resembling the untrilled German and French *r*.
13. A hard *k* sound produced at the back of the palate.
14. This sound is like the English *h* but has more body. It is made at the very bottom of the throat and pronounced at the beginning, middle, and ends of words.

CONTENTS

PUBLISHER'S PROLOGUE

Imām Ibn Rajab, may Allah have mercy on him, achieves in this book two major triumphs that speak to the modern Muslim intellectual condition. First, *The Heirs of the Prophets* deeply inspires in the serious reader—like very few books of human origin—the love and desire to gain true knowledge. It enlightens a people as to what realm of knowledge holds firm sovereignty over all the rest and is most vital for a true Islamic renaissance and revival. In recent years, Muslims have come to easily proffer that the *beneficial knowledge* praised by Allah and His Messenger admits any expertise that people attain to, including commerce, medicine, engineering, economics, and the like (regardless of one's intentions). These sciences are important, and many righteous scholars have commended them. However, they do not compare to that learning which leads men and women to the pleasure of Allah and salvation in the Hereafter. What worldly expertise can possibly compensate for the loss of knowledge concerning divine guidance to and along the straight path? What possible intellectual success can cover up for an ignorance that lures people into darkness and moral morass in this life and Hellfire in the next? The answers to these questions are obvious, but apparently not to everyone. Muslim countries, for example, continue to have universities that harshly tax their societies by placing their brightest students in the physical sciences and by relegating its mediocre students in "lesser fields," like Islamic studies. The shame of this is manifest, and its subtle impact on the minds of young men and women in the Muslim east is not minor. *The Heirs of the Prophets* is an eloquent and persuasive advocate of restoring our sense of priority when it comes to the acquisition of knowledge and, as a consequence, the conduct of our lives.

As for the second achievement, *The Heirs of the Prophets* unabashedly strips away any pretension as to what measures as true scholarship within the realm of Islamic learning itself. These pretensions have had uninterrupted breeding seasons over the years, to the point that it is difficult for most people today to distinguish between a preacher and a scholar, between technique and deep comprehension. For obvious reasons, this speaks especially to Muslims raised in English-speaking milieus, men and women who are vulnerable to being overly impressionable, on one hand, and vulnerable to overstating their own engagement with the Islamic sciences, on the other.

Ibn Rajab, in this very book, has fired a silver bullet that slays the superficiality that stubbornly persists. He says, "The uninformed person ... cannot conceptualize the essence of knowledge nor its sublimity.... One who fails to conceptualize something, its significance will never become rooted in the heart." *The Heirs of the Prophets* is a push-start to conceptualizing the utter importance of gaining *beneficial knowledge* so that it can be rooted in the heart of the Muslim body.

By translating this work, Imām Zaid Shakir has done, by Allah's grace, an important service to English-speaking Muslims who now have another opportunity to peer into the world of fine Islamic scholarship and be inspired to take the long and difficult path to attaining it.

TRANSLATOR'S INTRODUCTION

This modest project began in 1995, when I was blessed to obtain a copy of Ibn Rajab's commentary on a hadith narrated by Abū Dardā', *Al-ʿUlamā' Warathatu'l-Anbiyā'* ("The Scholars are the Heirs of the Prophets"). Having spent more than two years giving a series of addresses based primarily on Ibn Rajab's explanation of Imām Nawawī's *al-Arbaʿīn* (*Forty Hadith*), I was no stranger to Ibn Rajab's expansive exposition of a hadith's salient points. But there was something particularly moving and timely about Ibn Rajab's treatment of the famous hadith narrated by Abū Dardā'. I was inspired to translate the work into English, which I hastily did during the summer of 1995. My intention was to share a work that had touched me deeply with those brothers and sisters unable to read the original Arabic text. Unfortunately, the translation was quite bad, and it quickly found its way to the bottom of a stack of articles and personal papers I would transport with me during my travels between Syria and the United States.

During my years studying in Syria, the reasons that Ibn Rajab's commentary impacted me so greatly began to manifest themselves. Living around and studying with men who exemplified what Ibn Rajab was talking about in his book reinforced the importance of its major themes. Islam, as I was being taught, was an organic whole, comprised, at its most fundamental level, of three integrated components: *al-islām* (essential worship), *al-imān* (faith), and *al-iḥsān* (inner excellence). My teachers brought these concepts to life. For they were men most scrupulous in their worship, imbued with a deep and living faith, and most importantly, men who were firmly committed to upholding the torch of inner excellence in a way that made those around them believe that if they could not see Allah, they certainly were well mindful of His surveillance of their every breath—which is a level of cognizance that defines *iḥsān*.

These men were the righteous scholars Ibn Rajab was talking about. They were scholars who possessed both experiential knowledge of Allah and knowledge of Allah's commandments. They were scholars whose hearts were detached from the world; scholars whose erudition didn't prevent them from walking through the cold streets of Damascus immediately after Dawn Prayer to arrive at the homes of recently arrived students to teach them the most rudimentary aspects of *tajwīd* (proper Quran recitation) and jurisprudence. These men were truly heirs of the prophets. They were the type of scholar we so desperately need in North America, and they were the type of scholar we pray that Allah the Exalted blesses us to eventually become.

Being in the presence of such men stirred me to share my translation of Ibn Rajab's work with a few of my fellow students. The encouraging response of two of them, Ibrahim Osi-Efa and Osama Osman, led me to undertake the gradual overhaul of the original translation. When Osama left Syria to start a publishing house, I made an informal agreement to finish the revision of the translation so that it could be published as one of the initial projects of the fledgling Starlatch Press. The volume in your hands is the culmination of that process.

As I have previously mentioned, this work is particularly timely. As Dr. Abdal Hakim Murad mentions in the introduction to his recently published *Selections From Fatḥ al-Bārī by Ibn Ḥajar al-ʿAsqalānī*, the genre of hadith commentary has been largely neglected by English translators of Islamic literature. Ibn Rajab would certainly rank as one of the masters of this copious body of literature.

His commentary on Imām Nawawī's *al-Arbaʿīn* is considered by most scholars to be the best and certainly the most expansive. In addition to his unmatched treatment of Imām Tirmidhī's *ʿIlal* (*Hidden Defects* in hadith), he has written a commentary on Tirmidhī's *Jāmiʿ* (*The Compendium*), much of which has unfortunately been lost, as well as an incomplete commentary on *Ṣaḥīḥ al-Bukhārī* recently published by Mu'assasa al-Risāla of Beirut.

His expositions of individual hadith, such as the hadith of Abū Dardā', illustrate the breath of his erudition, the depth of his reflection, and his mastery of all of the major Islamic sciences, especially the science of hadith, an area where he was described by Ibn Ḥajar al-ʿAsqalānī as the "Master of his age in ascertaining hidden defects in hadith and investigating divergent chains of transmission."

Another of Ibn Rajab's salient qualities, which emerges in his commentary on Abū Dardā's hadith and other writings, such as *Laṭā'if al-Maʿārif* (*The Subtleties of Knowledge*), is his deep "spiritual" inclination. Like all of the scholars of his era, Ibn Rajab was well-versed in the science of *Taṣawwuf*, that is, Sufism. Although his writings in this regard would clearly be categorized as *ʿamalī*, or nonphilosophical, he is exacting in his usage of the nomenclature of this science. His confident usage of terms, such as *maʿrifa* (experiential knowledge), *zuhd* (complete indifference towards the world), *ʿilm al-ẓāhir wa'l-bāṭin* (outer and inner knowledge), and similar expressions, is done with the mastery of a person deeply convinced as to the validity of the ideas he is expounding.

Despite his manifest Sufi tendencies, in today's highly polarized and overly polemical Muslim world, Ibn Rajab would more likely be categorized as a *salafī*. Herein lies the greatest reason for the timeliness of this small volume. There are enemies of Islam who are striving their utmost to split the historical unity of *Ahl al-Sunna wa'l-Jamāʿa* (the community of Islamic orthodoxy). This unity has been predicated on the acceptance of four juridical schools, *Mālikī*, *Ḥanafī*, *Shāfiʿī*, and *Ḥanbalī*, and fostered by the acceptance of an approach in creedal matters that holds reason subordinate to divine revelation (*waḥy*), although scholars in the three former schools eventually came to accept the validity of applying reason and philosophical formulations as means to defend and prove the truth of revelation.

This position was generally respected by the *Ḥanbalīs*, except during infrequent periods of irrational intolerance. Similarly, the scholars of the three former schools respected the general inclination of the *Ḥanbalīs* in matters of creed (*ʿaqīda*) to cling doggedly to the textually informed approach of the people of hadith, even though this approach generally discouraged the use of rational proofs and philosophical formulations in matters of creed, thereby limiting the ability of its advocates to respond to the attacks and arguments of the proponents of deviant and alien creeds.

This dominant *sunnī* paradigm also was informed by an acceptance of *Taṣawwuf* as a valid Islamic science. This doesn't mean that anything bearing the label *Taṣawwuf* is beyond reproach. Ibn Khaldūn has shown in his *Muqaddima* how elements from *Ismāʿīlī* doctrine and aspects of alien philosophies were introduced into the compilation of teachings contemporarily known as *Taṣawwuf*. However, there has always been a basic corpus of doctrines and ideas that provided the foundations for a science of spiritual purification and character reformation which was accepted by all four of the juridical schools.

In this regard, the *Ḥanbalīs* are no exception. The most widespread of all the schools of *Taṣawwuf*, the *Qādiriyya*, was founded by the great *Ḥanbalī* jurist, ʿAbd al-Qādir al-Jilānī. His influence on subsequent major figures in the *Ḥanbalī* school, as George Makdisi has clearly shown, was to reach the great, if controversial scholar, Ibn Taymiyya, his student Ibn Qayyim al-Jawziyya, and his student Ibn Rajab. Their acceptance of the basic foundations of this science and their veneration for its early exponents helped to foster, even in this occasionally controversial area, mutual respect between the four schools Islamic jurisprudence.

This mutual respect, in turn, fostered a unified "paradigm"

which guided the intellectual and cultural life of *Ahl al-Sunna wa'l-Jamāʿa*, and it facilitated a unified and cohesive community. This unity is best exemplified in Damascus where the scholars and scholarship of the *Ḥanbalīs* have always been a vital part of the rich intellectual life of the city's vibrant *Sunnī* community. During the past century, the leading scholar of the *Ḥanbalīs*, Shaykh Aḥmad al-Shāmī, was one of the most respected and loved scholars in Syria.

That respect was similarly evident throughout history among non-*Ḥanbalī* critics of the dominant *Sunnī* paradigm. An example of this can also be taken from the recent history of Damascus. At the turn of the twentieth century, Shaykh Jamāluddīn al-Qāsimī emerged as the intellectual leader of a nascent "*Salafī*" movement in Syria. However, Shaykh al-Qāsimī situated his prolific and oftentimes critical writings within the dominant paradigm. His writings showed respect for both that paradigm and the scholars whose contributions were instrumental in shaping it.

Unfortunately, in recent years that paradigm has come under attack from within. This attack has been initiated by radical reformers whose strident rhetoric oftentimes signals their own ignorance of the very institutions they target. Leveling vicious, largely uncritical, polemics against the four juridical schools, *Taṣawwuf*, and the validity of rational proofs and philosophical formulations in creedal matters, these reformers are wittingly or unwittingly threatening the historical unity of *Ahl al-Sunna wa'l-Jamāʿa*.

In many instances, these reformers situate their attacks within the historical context of the *Ḥanbalī* school, relying on Ibn Taymiyya as their principal referent. This tendency has led in recent years to what could well be referred to as a neo-traditionalist backlash. Some defenders of the dominant *Sunnī* paradigm respond to the vicious attacks of the reformers with equal or surpassing venom. In their zeal, some go so far as to attempt to exclude the *Ḥanbalī* school from the ranks of *Ahl al-Sunna wa'l-Jamāʿa*. Others, while condemning those reformers who declare the likes of Shaykh Muḥyiddīn ibn

ʿArabī a nonbeliever, themselves declare Ibn Taymiyya to be outside the pale of Islam. If this polarization continues, our heartland—physically and figuratively—will be torn and divided to such an extent that we will never again be able to attain to the "critical mass" necessary to reestablish Islam as a dominant socio-political reality.

Individuals blessed with cooler heads must prevail. Ibn Rajab is an example of such an individual. He showed that it is possible to combine without conflict the constructs that have come to be known as "Sufi" and "*Salafī*"; that it is possible to be deeply committed to the *sunna* while simultaneously advocating and defending the four juridical schools; and that one can be critical of the formulations of the speculative theologians, while simultaneously respecting the institutional reality built by their followers. Ibn Rajab is truly an example of the complete, virtuous, and righteous scholar he mentions in this important book. He is truly an heir of the prophets. In these troubling and perplexing times, we are in dire need of luminaries of his kind.

A Brief Biography of Ibn Rajab

Imām Zaynuddīn Abū Faraj ʿAbd al-Raḥmān ibn Aḥmad ibn Rajab al-Ḥanbalī was born in Baghdad in 736 of the Muslim calendar. At the age of eight, he moved to Damascus along with his father. It was in Damascus that he began his religious studies. He first memorized the Quran in its variant canonical readings. He then began the study of hadith, a study which would take him to Makkah, Egypt, and other Islamic centers of learning. Ibn Rajab took from the leading scholarly authorities of his day. However, he was especially influenced by the great Ḥanbalī scholar, Ibn Qayyim al-Jawziyya. Although he was known to issue some legal rulings based on the opinions of Ibn Taymiyya, it isn't possible that he ever studied with him, as some people imagine, owing to the fact that Ibn Taymiyya died eight years before Ibn Rajab's birth.

Ibn Rajab was the leading hadith scholar of his era, an eminent Quran scholar, a jurist of repute, a moving sermonizer, and a major historian. His enduring literary legacy includes *Jāmiʿ al-ʿUlūm wa'l-Ḥikam* (*The Compendium of Knowledge and Wisdom*), considered by most scholars to be the best commentary on Imām Nawawī's *al-Arbaʿīn* (*Forty Hadith*); *Sharḥ ʿIlal al-Tirmidhī* (*Explanation of the Hidden Defects in Hadith*); a partial commentary on *Ṣaḥīḥ al-Bukhārī*; *al-Qawāʿid al-Fiqhiyya* (*Juridical Principles*); and *Laṭā'if al-Maʿārif* (*The Subtleties of Knowledge*), a beautiful compilation of the religious duties and invocations which correspond to the months and seasons of the year. He has written many comprehensive commentaries on individual hadiths, commentaries which amount to independent books. This includes his commentary on the hadith of Abū al-Dardā', the subject of this translation, and his commentary of the hadith *Bada'a'l-Islāmu gharībā...* ("Islam began unknown..."). Among his major historical writings is *Dhayl Ṭabaqāt al-Ḥanābila* (*Appendage to the Encyclopedia of Ḥanbalī Scholars*).

Given to solitude, deeply pious, and known for the abundance and intensity of his worship, Ibn Rajab passed from this world in Damascus in the year 795 AH. It is related that he went to a gravedigger a few days before his death and requested him to begin digging. When the digger completed his task, Ibn Rajab descended into the grave, reclined in it, then remarked, "Excellent!" A few days later, Ibn Rajab passed on and his body was brought to that very grave to be interned therein. Buried in Damascus, he left a rich heritage of knowledge. God willing, this book will introduce a small part of that heritage to the English-speaking world.

Introduction to the Translation

Good translating, owing to its highly nuanced nature, must be considered an art. Like all good works of art, a good translation is the product of a combination of the translator's God-given skills and the fruit of much practice. I don't claim to have an abundance of natural talent in this regard, and since this is my first complete translation, I do not have a wealth of experience. Therefore, I beg the reader's indulgence, while encouraging any and all comments and constructive criticism.

There are a few points which I feel will help the reader to maximize his or her benefit from this work. First of all, classical Arabic writing tends to be repetitious. This is due to the fact that many of the great works that have reached us were originally lectures, recorded verbatim by the teacher's students or professional scribes. If the teacher repeated a point for emphasis, or for some other reason, that point dutifully found its way into the manuscript.

This work illustrates that fact. Ibn Rajab repeats himself frequently. We have decided for the most part to leave those repetitions in the translation. Not only is it more intellectually honest, it also more closely conveys the spirit of the original work. Serious lessons are being imparted here. It should be our desire not only to read what the scholar said, but more importantly, to learn the lessons he is trying to teach us. Every serious pedagogue knows that repetition is one of the essential keys to successful teaching and learning.

Another aspect of many classical Arabic works is their lack of internal structure. Not only are chapter headings, sections, subsections, and paragraph breaks often missing, many works have no discernible system for indicating when one sentence ends and the next begins. Although in the days when most of our classical scholars were writing, the reader or listener's level of Arabic knowledge would provide that information intuitively. Today, that information usually comes as the result of numerous conscious decisions.

I feel that the decisions that informed my structuring of this work are good decisions, though they may not be the best possible ones. Therefore, if the work at times seems disjointed, don't let this lead you to an indictment of Ibn Rajab's thoughts, rather let it be an indictment of my decision-making in this regard.

There are two liberties which I have taken with the original Arabic text (critically edited by Ashraf ibn ʿAbd al-Maqṣūd and published by *Maktaba al-Turāth al-Islāmī* of Cairo). First of all, many Arabic proper nouns and attributions are preceded by the definite article *al-*. We have generally omitted that article, as this is the common practice in many English translations from Arabic. Hence, *al-Ḥasan al-Baṣrī*, *al-Bukhārī*, *al-Tirmidhī*, and *al-Madīnah* appear in the translation, as *Ḥasan al-Baṣrī*, *Bukhārī*, *Tirmidhī*, and Madinah. However, there are some instances where this article has been retained, as in *al-Shāfiʿī*.

Towards the end of the book, Ibn Rajab relates several biographical sketches, and then concludes the work with two poems. I have translated the poems first as an epilogue and then translated the biographical sketches in the form of an appendix.

If I have helped in any way to bring this work to life for the many English-speaking readers who will peruse its pages, it is solely due to Allah's infinite grace and mercy. Conversely, if the reader finds any serious problems with the work, they are strictly the result of my own deficiencies. In any case, we praise Allah for the innumerable blessings He has bestowed upon us.

In conclusion, there are too many people to thank for their help in making this work possible. They know who they are, and their reward with Allah is sure, *inshāAllāh*. There is one individual, however, who I must mention by name, Adnan Arian of Chicago, who provided advice, insights, and criticism which rescued this work when it was in its initial stage. May Allah reward him amply for the time, energy, and effort he sacrificed in that regard. It is my sincere hope that this will be just one of many fine works of The Starlatch Press.

Zaid Shakir
Albuquerque, NM
May 8, 2001

THE HADITH OF ABŪ DARDĀ'

A man came to Abū Dardā' while he was in Damascus. Abū Dardā' asked him, "What has brought you here, my brother?" He replied, "A hadith which you relate from the Prophet ﷺ." Abū Dardā' asked, "Have you come for some worldly need?" He replied, "No." "Have you come for business?" He replied, "No." "You have come only to seek this hadith?" He said, "Yes." Abū Dardā' then said, "I heard the Messenger of Allah ﷺ say: 'Whoever travels a path seeking sacred knowledge, Allah will place him on a path leading to Paradise. The angels lower their wings for the student of sacred knowledge, pleased with what he is doing. The creatures in the heavens and earth seek forgiveness for the student of sacred knowledge, even the fish in the water. The superiority of the religious scholar over the devout worshipper is like the superiority of the full moon over the other heavenly bodies. The religious scholars are the heirs of the prophets. The prophets leave no money as a bequest, rather they leave knowledge. Whoever seizes it has taken a bountiful share.'"

(Imām Aḥmad, Abū Dāwūd, Tirmidhī, and Ibn Mājah relate this hadith in their compilations.)[1]

Chapter One

TRAVELING FOR SACRED KNOWLEDGE

The early generations of Muslims, owing to the strength of their desire for sacred knowledge, would journey to distant lands seeking a single prophetic hadith. Abū Ayyūb Zayd ibn Khālid al-Anṣārī ؓ traveled from Madinah to Egypt for the purpose of meeting a Companion because he heard that this Companion related a particular hadith from the Prophet ﷺ. Similarly, Jābir ibn ʿAbdallāh ؓ, despite hearing much from the Prophet ﷺ himself, traveled a month to Syria to hear a single hadith. Without hesitation, such men would travel to someone of lesser virtue and learning in order to seek out knowledge that they lacked themselves.

A striking example of this sort of journey is what Allah relates in the Quran about Moses' ؑ journey with his young companion. If there ever existed a person who had no need to travel to seek knowledge, it was Moses ؑ, for Allah had spoken to him and given him the Torah in which all divine principles had been revealed. Still, when Allah informed him of a man (named Khiḍr) who had been favored with knowledge, Moses ؑ inquired about meeting him, and then set out with his young companion to find this Khiḍr, as Allah the Exalted says, *And behold, Moses said to his young companion, "I will not cease until I reach where the two seas meet, or I shall spend an exceptionally long time traveling"* (Quran, 18:60). Allah then informs us that upon meeting Khiḍr, Moses ﷺ asked of him, *"May I follow you in order that you may teach me of the knowledge you have been given?"* (Quran, 18:66). Details of their venture are related in the Book of Allah and in the well-known hadith of Ubayy ibn Kaʿb ؓ, which is related by Bukhārī and Muslim.

Ibn Masʿūd used to say:

> I swear by Allah, besides whom there is no other deity, no chapter of the Quran has been revealed except that I know where it was revealed. No verse from the Book of Allah has been revealed except that I know why it was revealed. Yet if I knew of anyone more learned than me in the Book of Allah, I would make every effort to reach him.[2]

Abū Dardā' ؓ said, "If I were unable to explain a verse in the Book of Allah and could not find anyone to explain it to me except a man in Bark al-Ghimād, I would journey to him."[3] Bark al-Ghimād is the farthest corner of Yemen. Masrūq ؓ went from Kūfa to Baṣra to ask a man about a Quranic verse. He failed, however, to find in him knowledge [about the verse], but while there, he was informed of a knowledgeable man in Syria. He then returned to Kūfa, from which point he set out for Syria seeking knowledge of the verse.[4]

A man traveled from Kūfa to Syria to ask Abū Dardā' about the validity of an oath he had taken.[5] Also, Saʿīd ibn Jubayr ؓ traveled from Kūfa to Makkah to ask Ibn ʿAbbās ؓ about the explanation of a single verse of the Quran.[6] Ḥasan al-Baṣrī ؓ traveled to Kūfa to ask Kaʿb ibn ʿUjra ؓ about the atonement for *al-adhā* [during the Pilgrimage].[7]

A thorough exposition of this issue—traveling to seek knowledge—would be exceedingly lengthy indeed. But to further illustrate this practice, a man took an oath, the validity of which the jurists were unsure. When he was directed to a man in a distant land, it was said to him, "That land is near for anyone concerned about his religion." This saying holds profound advice for one who concerns himself with his religion as much as he concerns himself with his worldly affairs. If something happens involving his religion and he finds no one to ask about it except a person in a far-off land, he would not hesitate to travel to him in order to save his religion. Similarly, if an opportunity were presented to him for some worldly gain in a distant land, he would hasten to it.

In the hadith under discussion, Abū Dardā' gave glad tidings to the person who traveled to him seeking a hadith he heard from the Prophet ﷺ regarding the virtue of knowledge. This is consistent with a statement of Allah, *When those believing in Our signs come to you, say, "Peace be unto you. Your Lord has made mercy incumbent upon Himself!"* (Quran, 6:54). Similarly, once a group of students crowded around Ḥasan al-Baṣrī, and his son then spoke harshly to them. Ḥasan said, "Go easy, my son." He then related this aforementioned verse.

Both Tirmidhī and Ibn Mājah quote Abū Saʿīd as saying, "Indeed, the Prophet ﷺ advised the scholars with good treatment of the students of knowledge."[8] Zirr ibn Ḥubaysh ؓ came to Ṣafwān ibn ʿAssāl ؓ seeking knowledge. Zirr said to him, "News has reached me that the angels lower their wings to the students of sacred knowledge." Abū Ṣafwān also relates this directly from the Prophet ﷺ.

One day people were crowded at the door of ʿAbdallāh ibn al-Mubārak, who said, "The students of sacred knowledge deserve the friendship of Allah and eternal bliss." He envied their gathering for this purpose because it leads to eternal bliss. For this reason, Muʿādh ibn Jabal ؓ cried as his death drew near and said, "I weep at how I will miss feeling thirst from the midday heat [from Fasting], standing in Prayer during the long winter nights, and the crowds of students kneeling around the scholars in the circles of knowledge."[9]

It is appropriate that the scholars welcome students and urge them to act on what they learn. Ḥasan al-Baṣrī greeted his students:

> Welcome, may Allah extend your life in peace, and may He enter us all into Paradise. Your seeking knowledge is a good act, if you persevere, are truthful, and are absolutely certain of the reward Allah has prepared for you. May Allah have mercy on you! Do not let your share of this good be such that it enters one ear and passes out the other. One who

hasn't seen Muḥammad ﷺ should know that the Prophet has seen him moving to and fro. The Prophet ﷺ did not erect tall buildings, rather, knowledge was given to him, and he dedicated himself to it. Do not procrastinate, salvation is at stake. What will make you heed? Are you hesitant? I swear by the Lord of the Kaʿba, it is as if Judgment Day will come upon you this very moment.[10]

Chapter Two

PATHS LEADING TO SACRED KNOWLEDGE

Let us now begin explaining the hadith of Abū Dardā'. "Whoever travels a path seeking sacred knowledge, Allah will place him on a path leading to Paradise." In another version of the hadith, it states, "Allah will make easy for him a path leading to Paradise."[11] Another version found in Muslim, related on the authority of Abū Hurayrah 🙏, reads, "Whoever travels a path seeking sacred knowledge, Allah will make easy for him a path leading to Paradise."[12]

Traveling a path seeking sacred knowledge can be understood as literally walking to the gatherings of knowledge. It can also encompass a more general meaning, like traveling an intangible path leading to the attainment of knowledge. This includes memorizing, studying, reading, making notes, comprehending, contemplating, and other acts which facilitate learning.

The Prophet's 🙏 statement, "Allah will make easy for him a path leading to Paradise," conveys many meanings. Among them is that Allah assists the student of sacred knowledge in his quest, placing him on its path, and facilitating his success. In these ways, the path of knowledge leads to Paradise. This facilitation is expressed in the statement of Allah the Exalted, *We have made the Quran easy to memorize. Is there anyone who will then be reminded?* (Quran,

54:17). Regarding this verse, some commentators say, "Is there anyone sincere in his quest for sacred knowledge that he might be aided in its attainment?"[13]

Many paths lead to Allah; among them is Allah's making it easy for the student of sacred knowledge to act on its dictates, if he learns it solely for the sake of Allah. Thus Allah will make it the cause of his guidance, will lead him with it, and cause him to act on it. These are all paths that lead to Paradise.

Furthermore, any student who seeks knowledge for the sake of sincere implementation, Allah will make it easy for him to gain additional beneficial knowledge. This is a path leading to Paradise. It is said, "Whoever acts on what he knows, Allah will bequeath unto him knowledge of that which he does not know."[14] It is also said, "The reward of good is the good it initiates."[15] This meaning is indicated by Allah's statement, *Allah increases in guidance those who pursue the path of guidance* (Quran, 19:76). And similarly, *As for those who accept to be guided, [Allah] increases them in guidance and bestows upon them piety* (Quran, 47:17).

Those who search for knowledge desiring to be rightly guided, Allah increases them in guidance and beneficial knowledge. This type of knowledge obligates righteous deeds. These are all paths that lead to Paradise. An additional path is Allah making it easy for the student of sacred knowledge to benefit from that knowledge in the Hereafter, to cross the Traverse [*Ṣirāṭ*], and to deal with the overwhelming horrors and imposing obstacles which precede it.

Knowledge is the Essence of Guidance

The reason the path to Paradise is made easy for the student of sacred knowledge, if he desires Allah and His pleasure, is explained as follows. Knowledge directs one to Allah from the most accessible paths. Therefore, one who travels its path, without deviating from it, reaches Allah and Paradise by means of the most direct route. The routes leading to Paradise have all been smoothed for him in this world and the next.

As for one who travels a path without knowledge, thinking it is a path to Paradise, he has chosen the most difficult and severe path. Such a person will never reach his destination despite tremendous exertion.

There is no path to experiential knowledge of Allah—leading to His pleasure and His nearness in the Hereafter—except through the beneficial knowledge which Allah sent down to His messengers and revealed in His scriptures. This [knowledge] guides to the right path. With it, clear guidance is sought out from the darkness of ignorance, ambiguity, and doubt. Allah has referred to His Book as a light with which one is guided through darkness: *There has come to you from Allah a light and a clear book. With it, Allah guides those who pursue His pleasure to paths of peace and He brings them out of darkness into light* (Quran, 5:15–16).

The Prophet ﷺ put forth a parable between the possessors of knowledge and the stars that guide people through the darkness. Imām Aḥmad relates (from Anas ﷺ) that the Prophet ﷺ said, "The similitude of the religious scholars on earth is that of the stars in the sky, by which [people] are guided through the darkness of the land and sea. If the stars are extinguished, even the guides might stray."[16]

This metaphor is penetrating, for the path to understanding Allah's oneness, experiential knowledge of Allah, His divine rulings, and His rewards and punishments are not attained through empirical knowledge. Rather, they are known through divine revelation. He has made this clear in His Book and on the tongue of His Messenger ﷺ. The scholars are the guides through the darkness of ignorance, ambiguity, and deviation. When these guides are lost, the travelers go astray.

The religious scholars have been likened to the stars, which provide three benefits: they guide [people] through the darkness; they adorn the sky; and they are missiles that repel the satans who ascend the heavens [endeavoring to intercept Allah's commands to the angels]. The religious scholars possess these characteristics: they guide through the darkness [of ignorance]; they adorn the earth; and they are missiles that repel the satans, who mix truth with falsehood and introduce heretical innovation in religion. Such innovations are introduced by people following their own whims.

So, as long as knowledge remains, people will be guided. But sacred knowledge will remain as long as the scholars remain. When the scholars dwindle in number, people fall into error. The Prophet ﷺ relates this meaning in a sound hadith:

> Allah does not withdraw knowledge by extracting it from the hearts of men, rather He takes away the religious scholars. When no religious scholar remains, people take the ignorant as their leaders; these ignorant ones are questioned and give religious verdicts without knowledge. They are astray and lead others astray.[17]

Tirmidhī relates from Jubayr ibn Nufayr ؓ, on the authority of Abū Dardā':

> We were with the Prophet ﷺ and he said, "There [will be] a time when knowledge will be snatched from the people until they will be unable to benefit from it." Ziyād ibn Lubayd said, "O Messenger of Allah, how will Allah seize knowledge from us when we recite the Quran? I swear by Allah, we recite it and teach it to our women and children!" He said, "May your mother be bereaved of you, Ziyād. I used to consider you one of the learned people of Madinah! The Torah and the Gospel are with the Jews and the Christians, yet do they benefit from them in any way?"[18]

Jubayr ibn Nufayr said:

> I met ʿUbāda ibn al-Ṣāmit and said to him, "Will you not listen to what Abū Dardā' is saying?" I then informed him of what he said concerning the loss of knowledge. He said, "Abū Dardā' has spoken truthfully. If you wish I will inform you of the first knowledge to be removed from people. It is humility [*khushūʿ*]. You will enter the central masjid and hardly find a single humble person!"

Nasā'ī relates a similar hadith from Jubayr ibn Nufayr, on the authority of ʿAwf ibn Mālik ؓ, from the Prophet ﷺ. He says in this hadith, "The Prophet ﷺ mentioned the straying of the Jews and the Christians despite their possessing scriptures."[19]

Jubayr ibn Nufayr also related:

> I met Shaddād ibn Aws and I informed him of the hadith of ʿAwf ibn Mālik, and he said, "He has spoken the truth. Shall I not inform you about the first occurrence of the lifting of knowledge? Humility will be lifted to the point you will not see a single humble person."

Imām Aḥmad relates a hadith in which Ziyād ibn Lubayd 🙵 mentioned something, whereupon the Prophet 🙵 said, "That will be in the time when knowledge is gone."[20] Ziyād mentioned this hadith and said, "Do not the Jews and Christians read the Torah and the Gospel without acting on it in any way?" In this version of the hadith, Ziyād did not mention the ensuing events contained in longer versions.

All of these narrations relate that the departure of knowledge resides in the failure to act on it. The Companions explained that the reason for this is the passing of inner knowledge from the hearts—with *inner knowledge* referring to humility. In this vein, Ḥudhayfa 🙵 relates, "Surely, humility will be the first knowledge to be lifted."[21]

Chapter Three

KNOWLEDGE OF THE TONGUE & THE HEART

Sacred knowledge, says Ḥasan al-Baṣrī, is of two types: "Knowledge of the tongue, which is the proof of Allah against the son of Adam, and knowledge of the heart, which is beneficial knowledge."[22] Ḥasan attributes this narration to the Prophet ﷺ, as Ibn Masʿūd relates in *Ṣaḥīḥ Muslim*, "People will recite the Quran, and it may fail even to go past their clavicles. Whereas, if it reaches their hearts and becomes rooted therein, it will be of tremendous benefit."[23] In this manner does beneficial knowledge touch the heart and impress upon it experiential knowledge of Allah, awareness of His sublimity, and humility towards Him. It bestows upon the heart exaltation, glorification, and love for Allah. When these characteristics settle into the heart, it is humbled; and the limbs, similarly affected, then follow in humility.

As related in *Ṣaḥīḥ Muslim*, the Prophet ﷺ used to say, "I seek refuge in Allah from knowledge which is of no benefit and from a heart which is not humble."[24] This indicates that knowledge which fosters no humility is of no benefit. It is related that the Prophet ﷺ used to ask Allah for beneficial knowledge. In another hadith, he said, "Ask Allah for beneficial knowledge, and seek refuge in Him against knowledge which is of no benefit."[25]

As for knowledge on the tongue, it is a proof of Allah against people. The Prophet ﷺ said, "The Quran is the proof of Allah for you or against you."[26] When inner knowledge departs, outer knowledge remains on people's tongues as a proof against them. This knowledge then leaves the possession of the scholars. Nothing then remains of religion except its name, and nothing of the Quran except its script. As for the Quran, it will remain in the books containing it, then at the end of time it will be raised from the books, and nothing will remain in the books nor in the hearts.[27]

Inner and Outer Knowledge

Scholars who categorize knowledge divide it into inner and outer knowledge. Inner knowledge is that which touches the hearts and instills in them fear, humility, awareness of Allah's sublimity, exaltation, love, intimacy, and yearning. Outer knowledge is that which remains on the tongue as a means for establishing the proof of Allah against people.

Wahb ibn Munabbih ﵀ wrote to Makḥūl ﵀, "Surely, you are a man who has attained the outer knowledge of Islam and thereby gained honor. So seek the inner knowledge of Islam and gain the love of Allah and nearness to Him."[28] Another version relates that he wrote, "Because of your outer knowledge, you have gained status and honor with the people. So seek inner knowledge to seek status with Allah and nearness to Him. You should know that each of these are separate stations." Wahb ﵀ indicates that outer knowledge is the knowledge of religious verdicts and legal rulings, the lawful and the unlawful, stories and admonitions, that which the tongue manifests. This knowledge gives its possessor love and veneration. In his letter, Wahb warns against stopping at what people give out and thus becoming spiritually stagnant and trapped into seeking people's love and glorification. One who stops at this has been cut off from Allah and deluded by people from pursuing Allah's pleasure. By inner knowledge, he means that knowledge which touches the hearts and instills fear, exaltation, and glorification. Wahb urged him to use that knowledge to seek the love of Allah and His nearness.

Chapter Four

CATEGORIES OF SCHOLARS

Many of the righteous forbears [*salaf*], such as Sufyān al-Thawrī
☙ and others, categorized scholars into various groups. The best
of these groupings is epitomized by the scholar who knows both
Allah and His commandments. By this expression, Sufyān refers to
those who combine inner and outer knowledge. These are the most
distinguished scholars. They are praised by Allah: *Indeed, among
His servants, it is but the learned who fear Allah* (Quran, 35:28).
He also says:

> *Indeed, those who were given knowledge beforehand, when Our signs
> are recited to them, they fall down prostrate on their faces, saying,
> "Glorified is our Lord. Indeed, the promise of our Lord will be ful-
> filled." They fall down prostrate on their faces, weeping, and it
> increases them in humility.* (Quran, 17:107–9)

Many of the righteous forbears used to say, "Religious knowledge is not an abundance of memorized texts. Rather, knowledge
is humility."[30] One of them said, "Fear of Allah is sufficient knowledge, and being deceived concerning Allah is sufficient
ignorance."[31] They further said, "One who knows Allah experientially does not necessarily know the commandments of Allah."
Such are the possessors of inner knowledge who lack adequate
comprehension of juridical matters. The righteous forbears similarly said, "One who knows the commandments of Allah does not

necessarily know Allah experientially." Such are the possessors of outer knowledge who have no inkling of inner knowledge; they neither fear Allah nor possess humility. They were deemed blameworthy by the righteous forbears. One of them said [concerning such a scholar], "This [type] is corrupt."[32] They stop at outer knowledge, while beneficial knowledge fails to reach their hearts. They will never savor its fragrance. They have been overwhelmed by their negligence, their hardness of heart, and their aversion of the Hereafter. They vie for the world, seeking exaltation in it, and are vainglorious.

The Harm and Enmity of Corrupt Scholars

Corrupt scholars think ill of those who have obtained beneficial knowledge. They do not love them, nor do they sit with them. They may even condemn them. They denounce them saying, "They are not real scholars!" This is from the treachery of Satan and his deception which prevents these corrupt scholars from attaining beneficial knowledge which Allah, His Messenger ﷺ, the righteous forbears of the Muslim nation, and its *imāms* have all praised.

For this reason, worldly scholars dislike righteous scholars, and they strive to their utmost to harm them, just as they endeavored to harm Saʿīd ibn al-Musayyib,[33] Ḥasan al-Baṣrī, Sufyān al-Thawrī, Imām Mālik, Imām Aḥmad, and other upright scholars (may Allah be pleased with them). This is because righteous scholars are the successors of the messengers, whereas worldly scholars resemble those who have earned the wrath of Allah—those who were enemies of the messengers, the slayers of the prophets, and murderers of the righteous. They are most intense in their enmity and envy towards the believers. Because of their intense love of the world, these corrupt scholars appreciate neither religious knowledge nor true religion. Instead, they glorify wealth, status, and positions of advantage with the rulers.

One of the ministers said to Muftī Ḥajjāj ibn Arṭā, "You know well jurisprudence and theology." Ḥajjāj said, "Why don't you instead say, 'You have honor and esteem?'" The minister said, "I swear by Allah! You belittle what Allah has extolled, and you extol what Allah has belittled!"[34]

The Deception of Satan

Many of those claiming inner knowledge speak about it, limit themselves to it, and condemn outer knowledge, namely, [the study of] the *Sharīʿa*, legal rulings, and matters concerning the lawful and the unlawful. And they defame its people, saying that they are veiled and are people of superficialities. This irresponsible attitude engenders vilification of the pure *Sharīʿa* and the righteous deeds that the prophets ﷺ brought, encouraged, and fostered.

Some of them go so far as to absolve themselves of the need to perform acts of worship, claiming that worship is for the masses. They claim that one who has attained [nearness to] Allah has no need for worship; in fact, such rituals are considered a veil for him. Junayd ؓ and others have said concerning such people, "What they have attained is only Hellfire."[35] This claim [that adherence to *Sharīʿa* is unnecessary] is from the greatest treachery and deception of Satan [Iblīs] towards those people. He will continue to play with them until he causes them to apostatize from Islam.

Among this group of deceived scholars are those who imagine that inner knowledge is not received from the lamp of prophethood nor from the Quran and the *Sunna*, but that it issues from personal impulses and divine inspiration. They entertain malicious thoughts towards the perfect *Sharīʿa*, thinking that it hasn't come with the sort of knowledge that rectifies hearts and draws people near to Allah, the Knower of the Unseen. This attitude ultimately produces in them a total rejection of what the Messenger of Allah ﷺ brought in this regard and leads them to talk about spiritual matters on the basis of conjecture and fancy. They are astray, and they lead others astray.

Examples of Virtuous Scholars

It is clear from this that the most complete and virtuous of scholars are those who are knowledgeable of Allah and His commandments. They combine the two [kinds of] knowledge, [the outer and the inward], which they receive from the Quran and the *Sunna*. They examine what people say on the basis of the Quran and the *Sunna*. That which agrees with these sources, they accept. And that which contradicts them, they reject.

These scholars are the elite of mankind—the best of humanity after the prophets. They are the true successors of the prophets and messengers. They were many among the Companions [of the Prophet 🕌], including the four righteous caliphs, Muʿādh, Abū Dardāʾ, Salmān, Ibn Masʿūd, Ibn ʿAmr, Ibn ʿAbbās, and many others. Similarly, from the generation after them, there were the likes of Saʿīd ibn al-Musayyib, Ḥasan al-Baṣrī, ʿAṭāʾ, Ṭāwūs, Mujāhid, Saʿīd ibn Jubayr, al-Nakhaʿī, and Yaḥyā ibn Abī Kathīr. And among those who came after the latter, there were people like al-Thawrī, al-Awzāʿī, Aḥmad, and others from the righteous scholars.

ʿAlī ibn Abī Ṭālib 🕌 has dubbed them godly scholars [*rabbāniyyūn*], indicating their praiseworthy status. Their kind is referred to in more than one place in the Quran. ʿAlī 🕌 says of them, "People are of three groups: righteous scholars, students of sacred knowledge, and the riffraff."[36] He then went on at length to describe both corrupt and righteous scholars. We expound on them elsewhere in this book.

Chapter Five

GRAZING THE GARDENS

In a well-known hadith, the Prophet ﷺ relates, "If you pass by the Gardens of Paradise, graze therein." The Companions asked, "What are the Gardens of Paradise?" He said, "Circles of *dhikr* [remembrance of Allah]."[37] Whenever he mentioned this hadith, Ibn Masᶜūd would say, "I do not mean gatherings of sermonizers, but study circles." A similar hadith has been related by Anas ibn Mālik.[38]

ᶜAṭā' al-Khurāsānī said, "Gatherings of *dhikr* are gatherings to study the lawful and unlawful, how to buy and sell, how to perform well the Prayer [*Ṣalāt*] and the Fast [*Ṣawm*], [the laws of] marriage and divorce, how to perform the Pilgrimage [*Ḥajj*], and similar matters.[39] Yaḥyā ibn Abī Kathīr said, "A lesson in jurisprudence is Prayer."[40] Abū Suwār al-ᶜAdawī was sitting in a study circle, which included in attendance a young man who exhorted the assembly to say, "*SubḥānAllāh* [Glory be to Allah!]" and "*al-Ḥamdulillāh* [All Praise is for Allah!]." Abū Suwār became angry and said, "Woe unto you! What then is the purpose of our gathering?"

This indicates that the gatherings of *dhikr* are not merely uttering the words "*SubḥānAllāh*, *Allāhu Akbar*, *al-Ḥamdulillāh*," and similar meritorious phrases. Rather, they include those gatherings in which the commands of Allah, His prohibitions, the lawful and unlawful, and that which He loves are discussed. Perhaps this latter form of *dhikr* is more beneficial than the former, since knowledge of the lawful and unlawful is obligatory for every Muslim in proportion to his needs. As for mentioning Allah with the tongue, it is largely voluntary and only rarely obligatory, such as *dhikr* in the mandatory Prayers.

What Knowledge is Mandatory for the Muslim

As for the knowledge of Allah's commandments—knowing what gains His love and pleasure and what incurs His anger—such knowledge is obligatory for everyone. For this reason it has been related, "Seeking knowledge is mandatory for every Muslim."[41] Hence, it is obligatory for every Muslim to learn the requisites of purification, Prayer [*Ṣalāt*], and Fasting [*Ṣawm*]. Furthermore, it is mandatory for everyone who has wealth that he learn what is obligatory in terms of Charity [*Zakāt*] due to the needy , doing what is voluntary and what is compulsory, Pilgrimage [*Ḥajj*], and *jihād*. Similarly, it is mandatory for everyone who buys and sells that he learn what transactions are lawful and which are unlawful. As ʿUmar said, "No one sells in our market except one who is knowledgeable of the religion."[42] A similar hadith has been related on a weak chain by ʿAlī who said, "Understanding of religion precedes commerce. One who engages in commerce without properly understanding the religion falls into usury with little chance of escaping from it."[43]

ʿAbdallāh ibn al-Mubārak was asked, "What knowledge is obligatory?" He replied:

> If a man does not have any wealth, it is not required that he learn the rulings of *Zakāt*. If his wealth reaches the *niṣāb* [minimum level of wealth that obliges one to pay *Zakāt*], it is obligatory that he learn how much he should give in *Zakāt*, when to give, and to whom. Other taxable possessions should be treated in similar fashion.[44]

Imām Aḥmad was asked about a man, "What knowledge is incumbent for him to seek?" He said, "The requisites for establishing Prayer and the divine commandments relating to Fasting and

Zakāt." He then mentioned the basic laws of Islam and said, "It is appropriate that he learn these." He also said, "Obligatory knowledge is that which is indispensable for performing his Prayer and establishing his religion."[45] You should know that knowledge of the lawful [*ḥalāl*] and unlawful [*ḥarām*] is honorable. It includes learning that which is individually and communally obligatory. Some scholars have written that learning the lawful and unlawful is better than voluntary worship, among them are Imām Aḥmad and Isḥāq.

Reluctance in Giving Religious Verdicts

The early *imāms* were cautious about speaking about [the lawful and unlawful], because one who speaks about such matters is relating information from Allah, enunciating His commandments and prohibitions, and passing on His sacred law. It was said about Ibn Sīrīn, "If he was asked about something regarding the lawful or the unlawful, his color would change. He would be transformed until he no longer seemed the same person."[46] ʿAṭā' ibn al-Sā'ib said, "I met people who, when asked for a religious verdict, would tremble as they spoke."[47] It is related that when Imām Mālik was asked about a legal matter, it was as if he were suspended between Heaven and Hell.[48]

Imām Aḥmad was extremely hesitant to speak on the lawful and unlawful, to claim that something was abrogated, or related matters which others would too readily expound. He frequently prefaced his answers with phrases such as, "I hope that...," "I fear...," or "It is more beloved to me...." Imām Mālik and others used to frequently say, "I do not know." Imām Aḥmad would often say on an issue about which the righteous forbears had various opinions, "The most likely answer is, 'I do not know.'"

Dhikr, Imān, *and* Iḥsān

Gatherings of *dhikr* also include gatherings of Quranic exegesis [*tafsīr*] and gatherings in which the way of the Messenger of Allah is related. Discussions that include the narration of hadith along with its explanation are more complete and virtuous than those involving narration only. These gatherings also include the discussion of all the legitimate Islamic sciences, along with their evidences and proofs. These sciences deal with outer knowledge and the inner knowledge of beliefs, constant awareness of Allah's watch over us, and the heart's perception of Allah's presence. The latter two comprise the constituent knowledge of *iḥsān* [excellence in worship].

These gatherings also include the knowledge of humility, love, hope, patience, contentment, and other states of the soul. In the hadith of Angel Gabriel ﷺ, *iḥsān* has been designated by the Prophet ﷺ as constituting [part of the] religion. Hence, understanding *iḥsān* properly is essential to properly understanding Islam.

The Two Circles

Such gatherings are better than gatherings whose *sole* purpose is to remember Allah [*dhikr*] by repeating the phrases, "*SubḥānAllāh*," "*al-Ḥamdulillāh*," and "*Allāhu Akbar.*" This is because learning one's religion is obligatory on either every individual or the community at large. Whereas, *dhikr* by extolling Allah is optional [in most cases].

One of the righteous forbears of Islam entered the mosque of Baṣra and saw that two circles were established. In one sat a sermonizer, in the other a jurist. He prayed a special Prayer in which he asked Allah's guidance as to which of the two circles he should join. He fell asleep then saw in his dream someone saying to him, "Do you consider the two gatherings equal? If you wish, I will show you the seat of Gabriel ﷺ in the circle of the jurist."[49]

Zayd ibn Aslam was among the most distinguished scholars of Madinah. He had a circle in the mosque in which he would teach Quranic commentary, hadith, jurisprudence, and other religious sciences. A man came to him and said:

> I saw in a dream an angel who said to the people of this gathering, "This host is secure in the Gardens of Paradise." Then he sent down to them a tender fish, which he placed in front of them. Thereupon, a

> man came to them and said, "Verily, I saw the Prophet ﷺ, Abū Bakr, and ʿUmar emerging through this door. The Prophet ﷺ was saying, 'Come with us to Zayd. Let us sit with him and listen to his teaching.' Then the Prophet ﷺ went, sat beside you, and grasped your hand."

It wasn't long after this vision that Zayd died, may Allah have mercy on him.

Despite what we have mentioned regarding the preference of knowledge to admonitions, the scholar must occasionally admonish people by relating stories to them. This is necessary to remove hardness from their hearts by helping them to remember Allah and His awesome power. The Quran includes this approach.

Hence, the learned jurist, in reality, is one who thoroughly understands the Book of Allah and implements it. ʿAlī ﷺ said, "The truly learned scholar is one who does not cause people to despair of Allah's mercy; nor does he give them warrant to rebel against Allah; nor does he leave the Quran, giving preference to other books."[50] The Prophet ﷺ himself applied this orientation. He used to encourage his Companions in his sermons, fearing that he would otherwise overburden them.

Chapter Six

ALL OF CREATION ASSISTING THE SCHOLAR

The Prophet ﷺ has said, "Verily, the angels lower their wings to the seeker of sacred knowledge, pleased with what he is doing." Ibn Mājah narrates a hadith related by Zirr ibn Ḥubaysh in which he said:

> I met Ṣafwān ibn ʿAssāl. He said, "What has brought you here?" I replied, "My quest for knowledge." He said, "I heard the Messenger of Allah ﷺ say, 'No one goes forth from his home seeking knowledge except that the angels lower their wings to him, pleased with what he is doing'."[51]

This narration is related by Tirmidhī and others directly from Ṣafwān.

Interpretations regarding the phrase "the angels lower their wings" vary. Some commentators interpret it literally, saying the angels spread their wings and extend them to students of sacred knowledge, carrying them towards their destinations on earth, helping them in their quest, and easing their acquisition of knowledge.

An atheist once heard this hadith and said to some students of sacred knowledge, "Lift your feet! Don't trample on the angels' wings and break them." He said this out of ridicule. As a punishment for these words, he remained fixed in his place until his feet dried and he collapsed.[52] In another narration, the atheist said, "They broke the angels' wings!" He then made himself a pair of nail-studded sandals and walked to the circle of knowledge. Thereafter, his feet became afflicted with gangrene.[53]

Other commentators interpret the phrase as meaning the angels lower their wings out of humility, as well as their subservience to the student of knowledge. This interpretation is derived from Allah's saying, *Lower your wing in humility to those believers who follow you* (Quran, 26:215). This opinion has validity in that the angels actually have wings.

Yet other commentators interpret it to mean that the angels surround the gatherings of *dhikr* with their wings overlapping one another until they reach the heavens. A similar interpretation is found in one of Ṣafwān's narration of the hadith, "The angels surround the student of knowledge with their wings, then they ride on each other until they reach the lower heaven exuberant by the student's quest."[54] Perhaps this is the weakest interpretation. Allah knows best.

Creatures Assisting the Scholars

[The hadith states],"As for the scholar, everything in the heavens and earth, even the fish in the water, seek forgiveness for him." Allah informs us in His Book that the angels seek forgiveness for the generality of believers. He says, *Those [angels] who carry aloft the Throne [of God], and those surrounding it, glorify the praises of their Lord. They believe in Him and seek forgiveness for the believers* (Quran, 40:7). He says also, *The angels glorify the praises of their Lord and seek forgiveness for the inhabitants of the earth* (Quran, 42:5). This forgiveness is comprehensive, extending to all believers. Yet all things on earth, even the fish in the sea, seek forgiveness for the scholars. Tirmidhī relates a hadith from Abū Umāma that the Prophet ﷺ said, "Indeed, Allah, the angels, the denizens of the heavens of the earth, the ants in their burrows, and the fish in the sea pray for blessings to come upon those who teach good to people."[55] Ṭabarānī relates from Jābir that the Prophet ﷺ said, "Everything, even the fish in the sea, seeks forgiveness for one who enlightens the people."[56] He further relates from Barā' ibn ʿAzzām, from the Prophet ﷺ, "The scholars are the heirs of the prophets. The inhabitants of heaven and earth love them. When the scholars die, the fish in the sea seek forgiveness for them from the time they die until the Day of Resurrection."[57]

It is related that such forgiveness is also sought for the student. Imām Aḥmad relates on the authority of Qabīṣa ibn al-Mukhāriq:

> I came to the Prophet ﷺ, and he asked, "What has brought you here?" I said, "My years have advanced and my bones are fragile. I have come to you in order that you might teach me something with which Allah will benefit me." He said, "O Qabīṣa, you haven't passed by a single burrow, nor a tree, nor a mud hill, except that its inhabitants sought forgiveness for you."[58]

The following verse is a further indication of this concept: *O you who believe! Remember Allah much, and glorify him morning and evening. He sends His blessings upon you, as do His angels, that He may take you from darkness to light. And He is merciful to the believers* (Quran, 33:41–43).

Allah and His angels send blessings upon the people of *dhikr*. And as previously mentioned, knowledge is among the best forms of *dhikr*. Ḥākim relates that Salīm ibn ʿĀmir said:

> A man came to Abū Umāma and said, "Abū Umāma, I have seen in my dream angels praying for your forgiveness every time you enter and leave, every time you stand and sit." Abū Umāma replied, "May Allah forgive me. Do not mention such things. If you wished, the angels would pray for your forgiveness." He then recited, *O you who believe! Remember Allah much and glorify him morning and evening. He sends His blessings upon you, as do His angels, that He may take you from darkness to light. And He is merciful to the believers.* (Quran, 33:41–43).[59]

Creatures of the earth

Some commentators explain that the beasts seek forgiveness for the scholars because the scholars spread goodness and mercy in the world. Also, the scholars command people to do good to all creation, even to slaughter in the most merciful way those animals that can be lawfully slaughtered. The goodness of scholars is thereby extended to the entire animal kingdom. For this reason animals seek forgiveness for the scholars.

Another meaning reveals itself to some commentators: animals are dutifully obedient to Allah and submissive to Him. They glorify Him and are not rebellious. Obedient beasts thus love obedient humans. That being so, what should their attitude be towards the scholar, who teaches people about Allah and the rights owed to Him and who calls to His obedience? Allah loves one who possesses these characteristics. Allah purifies him, praises him, and orders everyone and everything in the heavens and the earth to love and pray for him. In this way does He send His blessings upon the scholar. He places love for him in the hearts of His believing servants. Allah the Exalted says, *Indeed, those who believe and do righteous deeds, the Merciful will evoke love for them* (Quran, 19:96).

The Weeping of the Heavens and the Earth

Love for the scholar is not limited to the animate. In fact, inanimate objects also love him. This meaning is conveyed in the explanation of the verse: *Heaven and earth wept not for [the wrongdoers]* (Quran, 44:29). Commentaries on this verse mention the following narrations: "The sky weeps forty days for the believer when he dies." And, "The earth says to the believer when he is buried, 'You were the most beloved of those walking on my surface. You will see [my gentle treatment] when you are placed in my interior.'"[60]

Only sinful men and jinn hate the believer and the scholar because the rebellion [of the sinners and the jinn] against Allah requires that they place their obedience to their wild inclinations ahead of their obedience to Allah. Therefore, they hate obeying Allah and hate obedient people. Those who love Allah and obedience, love those who obey Him. They especially love those who call people to His obedience and command by the same call.

Furthermore, when knowledge appears on earth [due to the presence of the scholars] and is acted on, blessings abound and sustenance descends from the heavens. This benefits life for all, including ants and all other kinds of tiny creatures. This is due to the blessings generated by and for the scholar. The denizens of the heavens give glad tidings for the acts of obedience and righteous deeds that ascend from people on earth, and they seek forgiveness for those who are responsible for those deeds.

The opposite accrues to one who conceals knowledge that should be rightfully manifested. Allah, the angels, and the denizens of heavens curse the concealer of knowledge because he strives to extinguish the light of Allah. As a result of his concealment, sin, oppression, enmity, and tyranny appear on earth. Allah says, *Indeed, those who conceal what We have revealed of the clear proofs and guidance after it has been made clear to people in the Book, they are cursed by Allah and cursed by those who rightfully curse* (Quran, 2:159). It is said that this verse was revealed concerning the People of the Book who concealed the descriptions of the Prophet ﷺ contained in their scriptures.[61] Abū Hurayrah used to say, "Were it not for one particular verse in the Quran, I would not have narrated a single hadith." He then recited the above-mentioned verse.[62]

Barā' ibn al-ʿĀzib relates from the Prophet ﷺ, concerning the verse, *they are cursed by Allah and cursed by those who rightfully curse* (Quran, 2:159), "He informed us of those entitled to curse [these corrupt people]; they are the beasts of the earth."[63] This is also related directly from Barā'. A group of the righteous forbears have said about those who conceal beneficial knowledge, "The beasts of the earth curse them, saying, 'We have been denied rain because of the sins of the Children of Adam.'"[64] Concealing religiously beneficial knowledge leads to ignorance and sin. This results in the cessation of rainfall and in the descent of tribulations that afflict the beasts of the earth. They perish because of the sins of the Children of Adam, and they curse those who are responsible for their demise.

Chapter Seven

SCHOLARS AND WORSHIPPERS

It is obvious from the preceding chapters that love of the sincere scholars is an essential part of this religion. ʿAlī ﵁ said to Kumayl ibn Ziyād ﵀, "Loving the scholars is an act of worship." A well-known narration exhorts us, "Be a scholar, a teacher, a listener, or one who loves them. Do not be in a fifth category and thereby be ruined."[65] One of the righteous forbears said, "Glory be to Allah who has made for the people a way out."[66] This means that whoever abandons any of the first four praiseworthy categories necessarily enters a fifth and is thus ruined. He is neither a scholar, a student, a listener, nor one who loves scholars. He is therefore ruined. Whoever hates scholars, he loves their ruin. One who loves their ruin, loves for the light of Allah to be extinguished on earth and for sin and corruption to appear. This is consistent with what Sufyān ﵀ and others among the righteous forbears have said.

Once a servant of a ruler hated Abū Faraj ibn al-Jawzī and strived to harm him. One of Ibn Jawzī's friends saw the man in a dream being carried to Hellfire and inquired of the reason for such a terrible state. It was said, "Because he hated Ibn Jawzī."[67] Ibn Jawzī relates, "When the hatred and abuse [of this person] became unbearable, I sought refuge with Allah that He expose his weakness. Allah ruined him soon thereafter."

To Kill a Scholar is to Kill a Successor of the Prophet ﷺ

At the time that Ḥajjāj killed Saʿīd ibn Jubayr, the people were in dire need of Saʿīd's knowledge. [Ḥajjāj] thus prevented the people from benefiting from that knowledge. Then someone saw in a dream that Ḥajjāj [suffered the trials of] being killed once for everyone who fell during [his assault on Saʿīd]. For slaying Saʿīd, he was killed seventy times.[68]

This understanding is consistent with the idea that the most severely punished of people is one who kills a prophet, since the murderer has striven to work corruption in the earth. Whoever kills a scholar has killed a successor of the Prophet ﷺ and has likewise gone to great lengths to spread corruption in the earth. For this reason, Allah has specifically linked the killing of prophets and the killing of righteous scholars, *Those who reject the signs of Allah and unjustly kill the prophets and kill those who command justice, announce to them a painful punishment* (Quran, 3:21).

ʿIkrima ﷺ, as well as others among the righteous forbears, said concerning the following verse: *Whoever kills a human being, except as retribution for murder or corruption in the earth, it is as if he has killed all of humanity; and whoever saves a life, it is as if he has saved all of humanity* (Quran, 5:32), "Whoever kills a prophet or a just *imām*, it is as if he has killed all of humanity; and whoever supports a prophet or a just *imām*, it is as if he has saved all of humanity."[69]

The Full Moon, the Stars, and the Planets

The Prophet ﷺ said, "The superiority of the scholar over the devout worshipper is like the superiority of the full moon over the rest of the heavenly bodies." The meaning conveyed by this hadith has been related from the Prophet ﷺ by way of Muʿādh and Abū Dardā' with a broken chain of transmitters. This metaphor contains a comparison between the scholar and the full moon. The full moon represents the scholar, owing to the exquisite luminance of its light, while the planets represent devout worshippers. The difference in the radiance of the full moon and that of the planets represents the difference in virtue between the scholar and the devout worshipper. The underlying reason for this—and Allah knows best—is as follows: a planet's light does not extend beyond itself, whereas the light of the full moon shines upon the earth's inhabitants; they are illuminated by it and guided in their travels.

The Prophet ﷺ mentioned the planets, not the stars, because the planets are not used for guidance [as much as the stars]. Hence, they have the status of the devout worshipper whose benefit is limited to himself. As for the stars, they are the heavenly bodies that are used for guidance, as Allah the Exalted says: *And by the stars are [people] guided [through the land and sea]* (Quran, 16:16). He also says, *It is He who has set for you the stars that you may be guided by them through the darkness of the land and sea* (Quran, 6:97). In another hadith, the Prophet ﷺ also compared the scholars of his nation to the stars.

It has been said that the moon derives its light from the sun, just as the scholar is a reflection of the light of the divine message. For this reason he has been compared to the moon and not the sun. The Prophet ﷺ was a lamp and a luminous moon which shone upon the earth. The scholars, as his heirs and successors, are compared to the bright and luminous full moon.

Righteous Scholars: the First to Enter Paradise

The Prophet ﷺ narrates in a sound hadith, "The first contingent to enter Paradise will resemble the full moon; those entering after them resemble twinkling stars."[70] It is not unreasonable to say—and Allah knows best—that the righteous scholars are among this first contingent because they occupied the status of the full moon in the world. They are joined by the distinguished believers, those whose anecdotes are remembered, hearts are softened when they are mentioned, and their words are sought. As for the second contingent, they are the ordinary believers.

When al-Awzāʿī died—he was the *imām* of the Syrians in knowledge and was intensely fearful of Allah—a person saw him in a dream saying, "I haven't seen anything in Paradise greater than the rank of the scholar and the righteous sober individuals who fear Allah."

The Virtue of Knowledge over Ordinary Worship

The hadith of Abū Dardā' clearly indicates the preference of knowledge over ordinary worship. There is much evidence for this position. Allah says, *Are they equal those who know and those who know not?* (Quran, 39:9). He also says, *Allah elevates in degrees those who believe among you and those possessing knowledge* (Quran, 58:11). Ibn Masᶜūd and others among the righteous forbears have explained this to mean that Allah raises those endowed with knowledge degrees above the unlearned believers.[71]

Tirmidhī relates from Abū Umāma that two men were mentioned to the Prophet ﷺ, one of them a devout worshipper and the other a scholar. The Prophet ﷺ said, "The virtue of the scholar over the devout worshipper is like my virtue over the lowest of you."

Tirmidhī and Ibn Mājah relate a hadith from Ibn ᶜAbbās who related that the Prophet ﷺ said, "A single knowledgeable believer is harder on Satan than a thousand devout worshippers."[72]

Ibn Mājah relates that ᶜAbdallāh ibn ᶜAmr said:

> The Messenger of Allah ﷺ emerged one day and entered the Masjid. He found before him two gatherings. One engaged in Quranic recitation and invoking Allah, the other in scholarly discourse. The Prophet ﷺ said, "In each group there is good. These are reciting the Quran and invoking Allah. If He wills He will grant their request, and if He wills He will withhold it. These are engaged in scholarly discourse, and I have been sent as a teacher." He then sat with the latter.[73]

Ibn al-Mubārak, after relating this hadith in *Kitāb al-Zuhd*, adds, "The [latter] are better."[74]

Ṭabarānī relates from ᶜAbdallāh ibn ᶜUmar ﷺ from the Prophet ﷺ, "A little knowledge is better than abundant worship."[75] Bazzār, Ḥākim, and others relate from the Prophet ﷺ on the basis of numerous chains, "Copious knowledge is more beloved to Allah than copious worship, and scrupulousness is the best thing for your religion."[76] Zuhrī ﷺ attributes the following saying to the Prophet ﷺ, "The scholar is seventy degrees more virtuous than the devout worshipper. Between each two degrees is a distance that would take a swift horse a hundred years to traverse."[77]

The narrations from the righteous forbears on this subject are quite numerous. For example, it is related from Abū Hurayrah ﷺ and Abū Dharr ﷺ, "The least amount of sound knowledge is more beloved to us than a thousand units [*rakʿāt*] of voluntary Prayer." Ibn Mājah states that Abū Dharr related this directly from the Prophet ﷺ.[78] Abū Dardā' said, "Studying religious knowledge for an hour is better than spending a night in Prayer."[79] It is related from Abū Hurayrah from the Prophet ﷺ, "[Attaining religious knowledge] is more beloved to me than standing the entire night in Prayer."[80] Abū Hurayrah also said, "Knowing a ruling relating to a command or prohibition is more beloved to me than [fighting] seventy battles in the way of Allah."[81] Ibn ʿAbbās ﷺ said, "Studying part of the night is more beloved to me than spending its entirety in Prayer."[82] Abū Mūsā al-Ashʿarī ﷺ said, "Studying with ʿAbdallāh ibn Masʿūd is better for my soul than a year of worship."[83]

Ḥasan al-Baṣrī said, "Learning an aspect of knowledge and teaching it to a Muslim is more beloved to me than possessing the entire world and using it in the way of Allah."[84] He said on another occasion, "If a man correctly learns an aspect of knowledge and acts upon it, it is better for him than the entire world; even if he were given the world and used it all toward the Hereafter."[85] He also said, "The ink of the scholars and the blood of the martyrs flow in a single stream." He said, "Nothing which Allah has created is greater, in terms of its reward, than seeking knowledge, neither *Ḥajj*, nor *ʿUmrah* [Lesser Pilgrimage], nor *jihād*, nor *Zakāt*, nor emancipating slaves. If knowledge had a physical image it would be more beautiful than the sun, the moon, the stars, the sky, and a magnificent throne."

Al-Zuhrī ﵀ said, "[Seeking knowledge] is better that the worship of two hundred years." Sufyān al-Thawrī ﵀ and Abū Ḥanīfah ﵀ said, "There is nothing after obligatory worship better than seeking knowledge." Sufyān also said, "We know of no action better than seeking knowledge and hadith, if one does so with a good intention." He was asked, "What should his intention be?" He said, "He should desire Allah and Paradise."[86]

Al-Shāfiʿī ﵀ said, "Seeking knowledge is better than voluntary Prayer."[87] Imām Mālik ﵀ saw one of his students recording knowledge. The student abandoned his writing and stood up to perform a non-obligatory Prayer. Thereupon, Imām Mālik said, "I'm surprised at you! That which you stood for is not better than what you abandoned."[88]

Imām Aḥmad ﵀ was asked, "What do you consider better, that I spend the night in voluntary Prayer or that I record knowledge?" He replied, "That you record what you know of your religion is more beloved to me."[89] He also said, "Nothing is equivalent to knowledge." Muʿāfī ibn ʿImrān ﵀ said, "Writing a single hadith is more beloved to me than spending a night in Prayer."[90]

Chapter Eight

VIRTUE OF KNOWLEDGE

Among that which indicates the preference of seeking knowledge over voluntary worship is the fact that knowledge combines the virtues of all other acts of worship. Knowledge is the best form of *dhikr*, as has been explained. It is also the best form of *jihād*. It is related from ᶜAbdallāh ibn ᶜAmr and Nuᶜmān ibn Bashīr directly from the Prophet ﷺ, "The scholar's ink will be weighted against the martyr's blood and the scholar's ink will prove weightier."[91] Tirmidhī relates from Anas ibn Mālik that the Prophet ﷺ said, "Whoever treads the path of knowledge, he is in the way of Allah until he returns."[92] Another hadith relates, "If death comes to the student he is a martyr."[93]

Muᶜādh ibn Jabal ؓ relates:

> Acquire knowledge because doing so is good. Seeking it is worship. Reviewing it is glorifying Allah. Researching it is *jihād*. Teaching it to the ignorant is charity. Serving the scholars is a way of drawing near to Allah because knowledge is the path of ascension to the stations of Paradise. It is a companion in isolation and a comrade in distant lands. It speaks to you in solitude. It is a guide to prosperity and a shield against adversity. It beautifies one among friends and is a weapon against enemies. With it Allah elevates people and makes them guides and bellwethers of good. The scholars are people whose words are sought and whose actions are imitated. The angels long for the scholars' company and comfort them with their wings. Everything, the fish

> of the sea, the beasts of the earth, the predators of the land and sea, and the cattle pray that blessings come upon them. This is because knowledge enlivens the heart against ignorance, illuminates the eyes against darkness, and strengthens the body. It transports the servant to the mansions of the select and the righteous and to the highest ranks in the world and in the Hereafter. Contemplating it is equivalent to fasting, and reviewing it is equivalent to the Night Prayer vigil. With it, kinship is united and the lawful is distinguished from the unlawful. knowledge is an *imām* which leads to righteous actions. It is craved by the people destined for Paradise and shunned by people destined for Hell.[94]

This hadith has also been related by Abū Hurayrah رضي الله عنه from the Prophet ﷺ.[95]

The Virtue of Adam Over the Angels

The story of Adam عليه السلام demonstrates the virtue of knowledge over worship. Allah has shown Adam's virtue over the angels through knowledge, as He taught him the names of all things, while the angels acknowledged their inability to attain to that knowledge. When Adam عليه السلام informed them of the names, his superiority over them was manifested. Allah said [to the angels], *"Did I not say to you that I know the secrets of the heavens and the earth. I know that which you reveal and that which you conceal?"* (Quran, 2:33). Some commentators among the righteous forbears said that what [the angels] concealed was their saying to themselves, "Allah will not create anyone except that we are more noble than him."[96]

The superiority of Angel Gabriel عليه السلام over the angels who are preoccupied with worship is founded on the knowledge Angel Gabriel عليه السلام has been given. This indicates the superiority of knowledge. He is the dispenser of revelation to the messengers عليهم السلام. Similarly, the most distinguished messengers have been exalted over the other prophets عليهم السلام because of their heightened knowledge and reverence for Allah. For this reason, Allah has described Muḥammad ﷺ in many places in the Quran as being distinguished and favored with knowledge. The Prophet ﷺ, then, was commanded to teach his nation.

The first mention of a prophet receiving knowledge and being ordered to teach is found in the story of Abraham [Ibrāhīm ﷺ]. He prayed to his Lord for the people of his blessed household that He raise up for them a messenger from among themselves who would recite unto them His verses, teach them the scripture and wisdom, and purify them. He blessed us indeed by sending us a messenger from ourselves, Muḥammad ﷺ. Allah the Exalted says, *Allah has blessed the believers in that He has sent to them a messenger from themselves. He recites unto them His verses, purifies them, and teaches them the Book and wisdom, while before this they were in manifest error* (Quran, 3:164).

The initial revelation to Muḥammad ﷺ mentioned knowledge and its virtue. Allah says, *Recite in the name of your Lord who created—created man from a clot. Recite! And your Lord is most noble. He has taught by the pen—taught man what he knew not* (Quran, 96:1–5).

Allah frequently mentions blessing Muḥammad ﷺ with knowledge, such as Allah's statement, *Allah has revealed to you [O Muḥammad] the Book and wisdom, and He has taught you that which you knew not. Surely Allah's favor upon you is great* (Quran, 4:113). Allah commanded the Prophet ﷺ to request knowledge from his Lord: *Say, "My Lord, increase me in knowledge"* (Quran, 20:114). The Prophet ﷺ said, "I am the most learned and reverent of you concerning Allah."

Allah has blessed us by sending to us this messenger who teaches us what we lacked knowledge of. He rightfully orders us to give thanks for this blessing:

> *Thus, We have sent to you a messenger from yourselves; he recites unto you Our verses, purifies you, teaches you the Book and wisdom, and he teaches you that which you did not know. Therefore, remember Me, I will remember you; give thanks to Me and do not be ungrateful to Me.* (Quran, 2:151–52)

Allah the Exalted has informed us that He created the heavens and the earth and sent down the command in order that we know His power, knowledge, and attributes. He says, *It is Allah who has created the seven heavens and likewise the earth. The command descends between them in order that you may know that Allah has power over all things and that Allah encompasses all things in knowledge* (Quran, 65:12).

The Scholars Truly Fear Allah

Allah has praised the scholars in many places in the Quran. He has informed us that it is His knowledgeable servants who fear Him. They are the scholars. Ibn ʿAbbās comments on the verse, *Indeed, among His servants, it is but the learned who fear Allah* (Quran, 35:28), saying, "Indeed, My servants who know My majesty, grandeur, and sublimity fear Me."

The best knowledge is knowledge of Allah, His names, attributes, and actions. This knowledge engenders in its possessor direct knowledge of Allah, His fear, His love, His reverence, His exaltation, His magnification, intense devotion, absolute reliance on Him, patience, being pleased with Him, and preoccupation with Him.

This is followed by knowledge of His angels, His Books, His messengers, the Day of Resurrection, and related matters. Likewise, this includes knowledge of Allah's commandments, prohibitions, His laws, rulings, and that which He loves and that which He loathes of His servants' outer and inner actions.

Those who join knowledge of Allah with knowledge of His commandments are the righteous scholars. They are more complete than those whose knowledge is limited to experiential knowledge of Allah. They are also more complete than those scholars whose knowledge is limited to understanding legal rulings. Examples of such [complete] scholars are Ḥasan al-Baṣrī, Saʿīd ibn al-Musayyib, [Sufyān] al-Thawrī, Imām Aḥmad, and their like. Others who obtained this state are Mālik ibn Dīnār, Fuḍayl ibn al-ʿIyāḍ, Maʿrūf [al-Karkhī], Bishr [al-Ḥāfī], and others who had experiential knowledge of Allah.

Whoever compares these two states knows the virtue of those who have both experiential knowledge of Allah and knowledge of

His commandments over those who only possess direct knowledge of Allah. Therefore, how much better is one who has experiential knowledge of Allah and knowledge of His commandments over those who only have knowledge of His commandments! Their superiority is evident.

Some ignorant people think that devout worshippers are more virtuous than scholars. They imagine that scholars only have knowledge of Allah's commandments and that devout worshippers have experiential knowledge of Allah. Naturally, they consider those sages who have experiential knowledge of Allah more meritorious than the jurists who only possess knowledge of Allah's commandments.

We posit that scholars who have experiential knowledge of Allah *and* knowledge of His commandments are more virtuous than devout worshippers, even if these devout worshippers have experiential knowledge of Allah. This is because righteous scholars share with devout worshippers the virtue of possessing experiential knowledge of Allah. They may even surpass them in this virtue. However, scholars uniquely possess the knowledge of Allah's commandments and the honor of calling humanity to Allah and illuminating the path leading to Him. This is the station of the messengers, the successors of the messengers, and their heirs. This will be discussed later, God willing.

The knowledge that scholars possess is better than the supererogatory ritual acts of worship of the devout—acts of worship that some scholars may lack. Heightened knowledge of that which Allah has revealed to His Messenger ﷺ creates an increase in experiential knowledge of Allah and of faith. Experiential knowledge of Allah and true faith are better than the acts of the limbs. However, the uninformed person extols the importance of such worship over knowledge because he cannot conceptualize the essence of knowledge nor its sublimity. Therefore, he lacks the conceptual framework to attain the motivation to strive for knowledge. He can only conceptualize the essence of worship. He thus has the motivation to exert himself entirely in [his] devotions.

So you find many who lack knowledge preferring complete detachment from the world over engagement in the religious sciences and learning. As we just stated, such people cannot conceptualize the essence of knowledge and spiritual experience. One who fails to conceptualize something, its significance will never become rooted in the heart. In fact, an ignorant person conceptualizes the nature of the world and magnifies it in his heart. Therefore, he magnifies the virtue of one who leaves it. Muḥammad ibn Wāsiʿ once saw youth to whom it was said, "They are the otherworldly people." [Muḥammad ibn Wāsiʿ] asked, "What possible significance does the world have that merits praise for one who shuns it?" Abū Sulaymān al-Dārānī is known to have conveyed a similar point. One who takes pride in otherworldliness is like one who takes pride in leaving some trivial thing, something that has less significance with Allah than a gnat's wing. This world is petty and unworthy of mention, much less than something that evokes pride when it is shunned.

Many ignorant people extol supernatural occurrences and miracles and consider them better than the spiritual insight and knowledge given to the scholars. They conceptualize miracles [as a source of distinction] because they are manifestations of [a degree of] physical power and authority, which most people are incapable of. Supernatural occurrences, however, are not extolled as such by spiritually elevated scholars. They shun such occurrences, considering them a form of tribulation and trial. They expose the worshipper to the trap of veneration. The scholars fear preoccupation with [such occurrences] and becoming content with them and thus severed from Allah by them. Abū Ṭālib al-Makkī relates this in his book [*Qūt al-Qulūb*] from a large number of spiritual sages, among them Abū Yazīd al-Busṭāmī, Yaḥyā ibn Muʿādh, Sahl al-Tustarī, Dhū'l-Nūn al-Miṣrī, Junayd, and others. It was said to one of them, "That person can walk on water." He said, "One whom Allah empowers to oppose his whims is better off."

Abū Ḥafṣ al-Nīsābūrī was sitting with his companions one day at the outskirts of the city. While he was lecturing them—enthralling them with his discourse—a wild goat suddenly descended from the mountain and knelt down before him. Al-Nīsābūrī was visibly shaken and started to weep. His students asked him about his reaction, and he said:

> I saw you gathered around me and how enthralled you were. I thought to myself, "If only I had a sheep to slaughter and could invite you all to a feast." As soon as this thought occurred, this goat came and knelt down in front of me. Thus I thought, "Am I like Pharaoh who asked his Lord to make the Nile flow for him, and it was made to do so?" I then said to myself, "What can possibly protect me from Allah giving me every material good in the world, while I remain bankrupt in the Hereafter, possessing nothing?" This is what disturbed me.

The spiritual states of such sages is evidenced in the fact that they do not pay any attention to these supernatural occurrences. Rather, they are concerned with true knowledge of Allah, being humble before Him, [gaining] His love, nearness to Him, longing for His meeting, and obeying Him. The righteous scholars join [the spiritual types] in this, but surpass them through knowledge of the commandments of Allah and through calling humanity to Him. This is immensely virtuous with Allah, His angels, and His messengers. One of the righteous forbears said, "Whoever learns, acts on his knowledge, and then teaches it to others is considered to have attained greatness in the heavenly realm."

If the superiority of the scholar over the ordinary devout worshipper is clear, it should be understood that his superiority lies in increased knowledge. As for the devout worshipper lacking knowledge, he is denounced. The righteous forbears compared the latter to a vagabond; he does more harm than good. Such a person can be compared to a donkey turning a millstone; he goes round and round until he drops from exhaustion, having gone nowhere. This likeness is so clear that it requires no elaboration, and Allah knows best.

Chapter Nine

A PARABLE

We now present a parable regarding the states of humanity in responding to the Prophet Muḥammad's ﷺ call. Their states are many: one who is a sincere striver, one who is moderate, and a person who oppresses his soul. In showing how each group responds, this parable also reveals the virtue of righteous scholars over all other people.

A prophet is like a messenger who comes from a land belonging to a most magnificent king. He delivers the king's message to the rest of the lands. His fidelity to the message is manifest. The content of the message is as follows: there is no goodness as perfect as the king's goodness; no justice as complete as his justice; and no authority as firm as his authority. It is the king's desire that all of his subjects come to reside in his land. Whoever comes to him with a good record, he will reward him with the best of rewards. Whoever comes to him with a evil record, he will severely punish him. He will inform his subjects of all that they have done, good or bad.

The messenger thus travels to the far reaches of the kingdom, admonishing the inhabitants of those lands to prepare for the journey. He warns them of the imminent destruction of every parcel of land except the king's. He dispatches assistants to prod the wretched laggards who delay their preparation. He continuously describes the fine attributes of this king, [his] beauty, perfection, majesty, and generosity.

The people are divided into many groups based on their response to this messenger. Among them is one who believes him forthright. His only concern is seeking out what this king loves from his subjects to ensure that when he sets off [toward the king] he has an abundance of those things. He occupies himself with purification and calling on others as best as he could to prepare for the journey. He similarly asks about what the king loathes and then avoids it and enjoins others to shun it as well.

His greatest concern is asking about the attributes of the king, his greatness and generosity, all of which increases his love for the king, his exaltation of him, and his deep yearning to meet him. He eventually travels to the king, bringing [as gifts] the most precious and beloved things imaginable. His journey to the kingdom occurs as part of a grand procession. He knows from the messenger's instructions the most direct route to the king and the best provisions for the journey. Such is a description of the righteous scholars who are well guided and who guide others to the path of Allah. They come to the king as an absentee returning to his people. They await him with eager anticipation and the most earnest longing.

Another group is composed of those obsessed by their own preparation. They do not concern themselves with others. This is the description of the ordinary devout worshippers; they know what is beneficial and act on the basis of that knowledge.

Yet another group is made up those who behave as if they are included among the sincere people, as if their intention is to prepare for the journey. In reality, though, their intention is to occupy their condemned homeland. This group represents the scholars and worshippers who show off their deeds hoping to gain some temporal benefit. They are in the worst of states when they ultimately appear before the king. It will be said to them, "Seek the reward of your actions from the very ones you performed them for. You will have nothing here with us."

Another group consists of those who understand the messenger's dictates but are overcome with laziness and do not themselves prepare for the journey, neglecting what the king loves and indulging in what he dislikes. These are the scholars who fail to act on their knowledge. They are on the precipice of destruction, though they benefit others with their knowledge and their description of the path. Their students undertake the journey and are saved, leaving their teachers behind to be destroyed.

There is yet another group that believes the messenger's call, but fails to receive direction from him. These people fail to learn the details of the king's likes and dislikes. They undertake the journey guideless, and thus hurl themselves into roads rife with difficulties, horrors, wastelands, and disease. Most of them either perish or stray from the path, never reaching the king. They are ignorant believers acting without knowledge.

Yet another group is made up of those who completely ignore the messenger. They continue with their everyday routine, as if their homeland is not on the verge of annihilation. Some of them belie the messenger. Others confirm him with their speech, while ignoring his teachings. They are the generality of humanity, the masses who reject divine guidance and reject worship. Their ranks include the disbelievers, hypocrites, and rebellious fools who oppress and wrong their own souls. They feel that the caller has forced them onto the path, expelled them from their homeland, and unjustly summoned them before the king. They come before him as a rebellious slave comes before his angry master.

If you consider these divisions, you will not find any group more honored or closer to the king than the righteous scholars. They are the best of humanity after the messengers, may the peace and blessings of Allah be upon them all.

Chapter Ten

HEIRS OF THE PROPHETS

As for the Prophet's ﷺ saying, "The scholars are the heirs of the prophets," this means that they inherit the knowledge that the prophets taught. They succeed the prophets in their communities in the sense of calling people to Allah and His obedience, prohibiting rebellion against Allah and defending His religion. Ḥasan al-Baṣrī attributes the following saying to the Prophet ﷺ, "May the mercy of Allah be on my successors." The Companions asked, "O Messenger of Allah, who are your successors?" He said, "Those who revive and teach my *sunna* after my passing." A similar hadith is related by ʿAlī ؓ from the Prophet ﷺ.

The scholars occupy the position of the prophets in a noble station between Allah and humanity. This is as Ibn al-Munkadir ؒ has said: "Truly, the scholars are between Allah and humanity; therefore, be careful how you approach them."[103] Sufyān ibn ʿUyayna ؒ said, "The greatest people in rank are those who stand between Allah and humanity: the prophets and the scholars."[104] Sahl ibn ʿAbdallāh ؒ said:

> Whoever wants to look at the gatherings of the prophets, let him look at the gatherings of the scholars. Someone asks, "What do you say about a man who takes an oath against his wife to divorce her based on some condition." The unlearned replies, "His wife is divorced." Someone else comes forward with the same question. A discerning

man responds, "He should break this type of oath." This sort of question should only be directed to a prophet or a scholar.[105]

Noble Dreams Tell the Exalted Station of the Scholars

A pious woman during the time of Ḥasan al-Baṣrī dreamed that she was seeking a religious verdict concerning extra-menstrual bleeding [*istiḥāḍa*]. It was said to her, "You search for a verdict while Ḥasan is in your midst holding the Seal of Gabriel [Jibrīl] ﷺ?" This indicates that Ḥasan inherited the wisdom vouchsafed by Angel Gabriel ﷺ. This is known as the "Seal of Gabriel."

Someone saw the Prophet ﷺ in a dream and said to him, "O Messenger of Allah! We are at odds between Imām Mālik and Layth. Which of them is more knowledgeable?" The Prophet ﷺ said, "Mālik is the heir of my knowledge."

Another person dreamed that the Prophet ﷺ was sitting in the Masjid in the midst of an assembly, while Imām Mālik ﷺ was standing before him. In front of the Prophet ﷺ was a container of musk. He took it and gave it to Imām Mālik who then distributed it to the assembly. This was interpreted to mean that Imām Mālik was blessed with knowledge and strictly adhered to the *sunna* [the exemplary way of the Prophet ﷺ].

Fuḍayl ibn ʿIyāḍ ﷺ saw the Prophet ﷺ in his dream sitting down, and beside him was a gap. Fuḍayl advanced to sit there. The Prophet ﷺ said to him, "This is the seat of Abū Isḥāq al-Fazārī." One of those gathered asked, "Which of the two is better?" The Prophet ﷺ said, "Fuḍayl was a man who benefited himself with his devotions, and Abū Isḥāq was a man who benefited the public with his knowledge." This indicated that the latter was a scholar whose knowledge benefited other people. Fuḍayl was a devout worshipper whose benefit was confined to himself.[106]

The scholars will intercede on behalf of the believers after the intercession of the prophets, as Tirmidhī relates from ʿUthmān ﷺ a statement of the Prophet ﷺ, "On the Day of Judgment, the prophets will intercede, then the scholars, then the martyrs."[107]

Mālik ibn Dīnār ﵀ said, "I have heard that it will be said to the devout [on the Day of Judgment], 'Enter Paradise!' While it will be said to the scholar, 'Rise and intercede!'" This narration, however, is related from Abū Hurayrah with a very weak chain.[108]

The scholars will be a proof at the Gathering Station [*al-Maḥshar*] during the tumult of the Day of Judgment. The people gathered there will think that they only stayed in their graves a brief time. The scholars will make it clear that the truth is to the contrary. Allah the Exalted says:

> *On the day that the Hour is established, the criminal transgressors will swear that they only tarried a brief time. Thus were they deluded from the truth. Whereas those given knowledge and faith will say, "You tarried, in accordance to Allah's Book of decree, until the Day of Resurrection."* (Quran, 30:55–56)

The scholars will also comment on the debasement of the idolaters on the Day of Judgment, as Allah says: *On the Day of Resurrection, He will debase [the idolaters] and say, "Where are My partner gods that you used to dispute [the believers] about?" Those given knowledge will say, "Debasement and evil this day are upon those who reject faith!"* (Quran, 16:27).

It has been related from the Prophet ﷺ, "People will need scholars in Paradise just as they need them in the world. When the Lord summons the people of Paradise to stand before Him, He will say to them, 'Ask what you desire.' They will turn to the scholars, who will say, 'Ask Him to enable you to see Him. What in Paradise is greater than that!'" All of these narrations make it clear that there is no rank after prophethood better than that of the scholars.

Scholars, the Befriended of Allah

The Quran relates, *Allah bears witness that there is no God but Him, as do the angels and those endowed with knowledge* (3:18). In this verse, the prophets have not been mentioned individually, but inclusively with the scholars. This is sufficient honoring of the scholars in that they have been mentioned in a way that includes the prophets ﵈. This is the basis of those who say, "The scholars who act on their knowledge are the protected friends of Allah." Both Abū Ḥanīfah ﵁ and al-Shāfiʿī ﵁ have said, "If the scholars and jurists are not the protected friends of Allah, then Allah has no such friends."[109] Imām Aḥmad ﵁ said, "The people of hadith are the *abdāl* [people of superior piety]."[110]

The Prophet ﷺ said, "Indeed, the prophets do not leave money as an inheritance. Rather, they leave knowledge. Whoever seizes it has taken a bountiful share indeed." So knowledge is the heritage of the prophets, which means that the scholars are the heirs to what the prophets leave behind, namely, beneficial knowledge. Whoever seizes it and prizes it has obtained a great fortune, which his companions can rightfully envy. Ibn Masʿūd saw a group of people studying in the Prophet's Masjid. A man said, "Why have they gathered? He said, "They have gathered for the inheritance of Muḥammad ﷺ; they are distributing it among themselves," [that is, distributing knowledge]. Once Abū Hurayrah headed toward the market. Upon leaving, he said to his family, "You abandon the inheritance of Muḥammad ﷺ being distributed in the Masjid and remain here! His heritage is the Quran, as well as the *Sunna* that explains and makes clear its meanings."[111]

It is related in *Ṣaḥīḥ al-Bukhārī* that Ibn ʿAbbās was asked, "Did the Prophet ﷺ leave anything?" He said, "He did not leave anything except what is between the two covers [of the Book]," that is, the Quran.[112] It is related in *Ṣaḥīḥ al-Bukhārī* and *Ṣaḥīḥ Muslim* that Ibn Abū Awfā was asked, "Did the Prophet bequeath anything?" He said, "He bequeathed the Quran."[113] The Prophet ﷺ gave a sermon after the Farewell Pilgrimage and said:

> I am but a mortal being. The [Angel of Death] is about to come to me, and I will respond to his summon. I am leaving with you two weighty things. The first is the Book of Allah, in which there is guidance and light. Whoever seizes hold of it and takes it, he will be guided. Whoever lets it escape, he will go astray.[114]

Imām Aḥmad relates that ʿAbdallāh ibn ʿAmr said:

> The Prophet ﷺ came out to us and said, "I am the unlettered Prophet." He said this three times. [He then continued], "There is no prophet

> after me. I have been given speech that is decisive and comprehensive. I have learned the number of the guardians of Hellfire and the number of angels bearing the lofty Throne [of Allah]. The faults of my nation have been wiped out. Therefore, listen well and obey me as long as I am with you. When I am taken away, you must adhere to the Book of Allah. Hold as lawful that which it legislates as lawful, and hold as unlawful that which it prohibits." Then he said, "The prophets do not leave money as an inheritance. Rather, they leave knowledge."[115]

The Prophet ﷺ means by this that they do not leave anything except knowledge. This is consistent with the verse, *Solomon was the heir of David* (Quran, 27:16); and His statement concerning Zachariah [Zakariyya ﷺ], *And bestow upon me an heir who will receive my heritage and the heritage of the family of Jacob* (Quran, 19:5–6). What is intended here is the heritage of knowledge and prophecy, not material wealth. The prophets ﷺ did not accumulate material belongings that can be left behind in worldly bequest.

The Prophet ﷺ said, "Whatever I leave behind other than provision for my servant and maintenance for my family, it is charity."[116] He did not leave anything behind except a coat of armor, his weapon, his white mule, and a piece of land, which he gave in charity.[117] [In a similar narration] it is mentioned that the Prophet ﷺ did not leave behind anything except a single tool and land that he and his family used to grow their food. He gave it to the Muslims in charity.

All of this indicates that the messengers ﷺ were not sent to gather worldly possessions for their families. Rather, they were sent to call people to Allah, struggle in His path, disseminate beneficial knowledge, and leave that knowledge as a bequest for their communities.

Abū Muslim al-Khūlānī attributes [the following saying] to the Prophet ﷺ: "Allah did not inspire me to collect wealth and be a merchant. Rather, He revealed to me, *Glorify the praises of your Lord and be among those who prostrate themselves [unto Him]; and worship your Lord until death comes to you* (Quran, 15:99)."[118] Tirmidhī and others relate that the Prophet ﷺ said,

"What do I have to do with the world! The similitude of myself and the world is like a rider; he seeks shade briefly under a tree, rises, and moves on."[119]

Hence, the Prophet ﷺ said, "The religious scholars are the heirs of the prophets. The prophets do not leave money as an inheritance. Rather, they leave knowledge."[120] In this part of the hadith two things are alluded to. First, the scholar is the true heir of the Messenger. Just as the scholar has inherited the Messenger's knowledge, it is fitting that he leave a heritage of knowledge as the Messenger ﷺ did. The scholar's heritage is what he leaves behind through teaching, writing, and other endeavors which benefit people after him. The Prophet ﷺ said, "When the servant dies his actions are cut off except for three things: beneficial knowledge, continuous charity, or a righteous son who prays for him."[121] If the scholar teaches one who acts on his knowledge after him, he has left behind beneficial knowledge and continuous charity. Teaching is a form of charity, as has been related previously from Muʿādh and others. Those people whom the scholar taught have a status equivalent to his righteous children; they pray for him. Therefore, they confer upon him all three of these distinctions because of the knowledge he left.

As for the second point, the scholar does not leave behind any worldly thing, just as the Messenger ﷺ did not. This is the scholar's way, owing to his exactness following the prophets. This scrupulousness is encompassed in his following the Messenger ﷺ and his *sunna*, turning away from the world, taking little from it, and being content with that. Sahl al-Tustarī ؓ used to say, "Among the signs of the love of the *sunna* is the love of the Hereafter, dislike of the world, and not indulging in anything except sufficient provision for the Hereafter."

Epilogue

A POEM ON PROTECTING KNOWLEDGE

Abū al-Ḥasan ʿAbd al-ʿAzīz al-Jurjānī said:

They say to me that you are withdrawn,
but they saw a man even more humiliated and withdrawn.
I saw people who belittled any humble soul who drew near to them;
anyone who was exalted by pride they received with honor.
I gave not knowledge its due,
and every time a craving for the world came to me,
I used my knowledge as a staircase to attain it.
When it was said, "This is a fountain." I said, "I see."
But the unfettered soul will [foolishly] endure thirst.

I strove not in the service of knowledge,
nor as a servant of the needy souls I met.
I sought, instead, to be served.
Am I to be made wretched by the seedling I planted,
harvesting only humiliation?
If this is so, it would have been better to have sought ignorance!
If only the people of knowledge had protected it,
it would have protected them.

If they had magnified it in their souls,
they would have been magnified.
To the contrary, they belittled it,
and thereby became despicable.
They disfigured its face with their craving for the world,
leaving it frowning and dejected.

A Poem on Repentance and Returning to Allāh

The time has come for me to see after the darkness of ignorance.
My old age is a morning that calls me to its dawning rays.
The night of youth is short, so proceed deliberately.
The morning is the end of the road for the night traveler.
How have I been deceived by the world and its adornment,
building my home on the crumbling ground, at the edge of a precipice?
A home whose transgressions remain, but whose delights perish:
How wretched is such a home!
The happy one is not one who is delighted by his worldly trinkets.
Rather, the happy one is one saved from the torment of Hell.

I have awakened from my wickedness, fearful and trembling,
for Allah knows my deeds, open and secret.
If I hold my sins to be grave and they fill me with despair,
I can only hope that they will be eradicated,
by the One who alone can do so ...
The All-Forgiving.

Appendix

THE ABSTINENCE OF THE EARLY SCHOLARS

Mālik ibn Dīnār ؓ said, "If you come to the scholar's house and do not find him, his house tells a story. You see his prayer mat, his copy of the Quran, and the washroom on the side of his house. You discern a trace of the Hereafter."[122]

About Fuḍayl ibn ʿIyāḍ ؓ
Fuḍayl used to say, "Beware of the worldly scholar so that he does not turn you away [from the path of righteousness] with his drunkenness. Many of your scholars, their clothes more closely resemble the clothes of Khosrau and Caesar than those of Muḥammad ﷺ. Muḥammad ﷺ did not erect tall buildings. Instead knowledge was given to him and he dedicated himself to it."[123] He also used to say, "Scholars are many, but wise men are few. The essence of knowledge is wisdom. Whoever is given wisdom has been given abundant good." Such was the state of the righteous scholars such as Ḥasan al-Baṣrī ؓ, Sufyān al-Thawrī ؓ, and Imām Aḥmad ؓ. They were content with a little from the world, to the point that they departed from it not leaving anything except knowledge. This is despite the fact that some of them used to wear nice clothes or eat descent food, removed from asceticism.

About Ḥasan al-Baṣrī

He used to eat meat every day. He used to buy a piece of meat for half a dirham, cook it in a tasty broth, and share it with his family. He would feed anyone who came to him. He used to wear nice garments. Despite this, he was the most otherworldly of people. He wouldn't strive for any worldly thing. When people sat with him, they would leave divorced from the world. They did not know anyone who despised worldly people more than he.[124] They used to visit him during his illness and found nothing in his house, great or small, except a cushion wrapped up around him. Ibn ʿAwn said, "Ḥasan monopolized otherworldliness for himself; he shared knowledge with the people." Ḥasan himself used to say, "The scholar turns away from the world, longs for the Hereafter, exerts himself in worship, and implements the *sunna* of Muḥammad."[125]

About Sufyān al-Thawrī

Sufyān al-Thawrī was more austere in his dress than Ḥasan [al-Baṣrī]. One who did not know him would think he was a beggar upon seeing him. Despite the depth of his scrupulousness, if he found some lawful food he would eat heartily from it. If he found nothing lawful to eat, he would swallow sand. He might go three days without eating anything despite people offering him abundant wealth. If he became satiated from lawful food he would increase his worship. He was the most otherworldly of people in his time, his gatherings were stripped of any worldly pretensions. No one was more humble than the sultans, kings, and wealthy in his gatherings; and no one more dignified than the poor and indigent. He was overwhelmed by the fear of Allah's wrath. When he was afflicted with the disease that would eventually kill him, his urine was carried to a doctor who said, "There is no cure for this disease. Sadness and fear have shattered his liver."[126] It is said that there was no one in his era more fearful of Allah than him, and no one more awestruck before Allah. When he died, one of the scholars said, "O people of extravagance, consume the world at the expense of your religion. Sufyān has died." He meant by this that no one remained who inspired shyness and restraint.

About Imām Aḥmad ibn al-Ḥanbal

He was even more ascetic [than Sufyān]. He lived simply and patiently endured difficult conditions. His livelihood was from some stores which he inherited from his father. The income he took from them was less than twenty dirhams a month. He died and did not leave anything other than a few pieces of silver wrapped in a rag, the weight of which was less than half a dirham. He left a debt that was paid for from his stores, despite the abundant wealth offered to him by rulers.[127]

About Imām Yaḥyā ibn Abī Kathīr

Yaḥyā ibn Abī Kathīr was among the extremely knowledgeable righteous scholars. It was said, "There does not remain on the face of the earth the likes of him." He was well-kept and well-dressed, but when he died, he only left thirty silver coins which were used to pay for his burial shroud.

About Imām Muḥammad ibn Aslam al-Ṭūsī

Muḥammad ibn Aslam al-Ṭūsī was among the otherworldly righteous scholars. He died and did not leave anything except his garment and skullcap. They placed them on his bier. He also left a vessel for making ablution [*wuḍū'*], which was given away in charity. The women gathered on their roofs during his funeral and said, "This scholar who has passed from the world, his bequest [is these few things] on his bier. He isn't like our [other] scholars. They are slaves of their stomachs. One of them sits two or three years teaching and gains nothing but loss, benefiting only in worldly goods."[128]

About Imām al-Awzāʿī

ʿAbbās ibn Muraththad said, "I heard our companions saying,

'More than seventy thousand *dinārs* came to al-Awzāʿī from the Umayyid rulers. When he died he only left behind seven *dinārs*. He had neither land nor a home.'"[129] ʿAbbās then said, "We investigated and found that he spent it all in the way of Allah and the poor."

Allah, in His Book, has described the scholars as possessing many characteristics. Among them are the fear of Allah, humility, and weeping. Also among them is belittling the world and turning away from it. He illustrates this in the story of Qārūn [Korah]:

> *He came out before his people in all of his adornments. Those who desire the life of this world said, "If only we were to have what Qārūn was given! He has a great fortune indeed!" And those who had been given knowledge said, "Woe unto you people! Allah's good reward is better for those who believe and do righteous deeds. And only the patient shall receive it."* (Quran, 28:79–80)

It was mentioned to Imām Aḥmad that it was said to Ibn al-Mubārak, "How does one know a truthful scholar?" He said, "[He] turns away from money and moves towards the Hereafter." Imām Aḥmad said, "Yes, such should be his state." Imām Aḥmad used to rebuke scholars for loving the world and longing for it. You should know that scholars are ruined. When [scholars] start aspiring for the world, they cause the ignorant to think ill of them and cause them to set up ignorant people as their leaders.[130]

ʿAlī 豢 saw a popular preacher and said to him, "I will question you about an issue. If you do not answer correctly, refrain from preaching. Otherwise, I'll give you this gem." The preacher said, "Ask." ʿAlī then said, "What buttresses religion and what eradicates it?" He said, "Scrupulousness is the buttress of religion and aspiring for the world eradicates it." ʿAlī 豢 said, "Continue preaching. People like you are fit to do so."[131] This question from ʿAlī 豢 indicates that it is fitting for one who admonishes people to refrain from their possessions, not to covet wealth and provisions, and not to try to win their hearts. Rather he should spread knowledge for the sake of Allah and not ask the people for anything out of piety.

Ibn Mājah relates that Ibn Masʿūd 豢 said:

> If scholars safeguarded knowledge and placed it with its proper people, they would have dominated their epoch. Instead, they expended it on worldly people, in order to obtain something of their possessions. These worldly people then scorned them. I heard your Prophet ﷺ say: "Whoever narrows his concerns into a single concern, let him be concerned with the Hereafter. Allah will suffice him in his worldly affairs." One torn by his worldly concerns will not even notice how Allah is destroying him.[132]

Therefore, craving for the world and aspiring for it is despicable. It is even more despicable in a scholar. When it occurs in an elderly scholar it is even viler.

One of the scholars among the Successors [*Tābiʿīn*][A] donned his garment and prepared to visit a king. He took a mirror, looked into it, saw his graying beard, and said, "I'm worried about [impressing] the king, and my beard is graying!" He then took off his garment and sat down.

Abū Ḥāzim ؓ said, "We experienced a brief time in our era when not a single scholar sought out a ruler. If a man was learned, he was satisfied with knowledge and needed nothing else. In this situation, there was benefit for both parties. When the rulers saw that the scholars covered their faults, sat in their company, and begged for their possessions, they despised them, stopped taking their advise, and [stopped] seeking their knowledge. This led to the ruin of both parties."

More about Ḥasan al-Baṣrī ؓ

A desert Arab came to Baṣra and asked, "Who is the leader of this town?" They said, "Ḥasan." He inquired, "With what does he rule? They said, "The people need his knowledge, and he has nothing to do with their possessions." Ḥasan used to say, "Everything can be defaced, and the defacement of knowledge is greed." He also said, "One who increases in knowledge and simultaneously

---

[A] Successors (*Tābiʿīn*) are those very early Muslims who lived immediately after the time of the Prophet ﷺ and who made contact with any of the Prophet's Companions.

increases in worldly longing, will only increase in distancing himself from Allah, and Allah will increase in dislike of him."[133]

One day Ḥasan saw some of the Quran reciters at the gates of a palace. He said:

> You have wrinkled your foreheads, flattened your mules [loaded with provisions], and come here carrying knowledge to their doors. Now they will have nothing to do with you. If you were to stay in your homes until they sent for you, it would have been better for you. Leave! May Allah distance you from them!

In another version, it reads:

> Leave! May Allah separate between your spirits. You have flattened your mules, tucked up the ends of your garments, and disheveled your hair. While you have sought their possessions, they will have nothing to do with you. You have disgraced the Quran reciters, may Allah disgrace you. I swear by Allah, if you were to ignore their possessions, they would have sought your knowledge. You have instead sought their possessions, while they have shunned you and your knowledge. May Allah distance the one who distances himself.

In summary, the scholar who does not defend his honor will not benefit from his knowledge; nor will others. Al-Shāfiʿī said:

> Whoever recites the Quran, his value is amplified. Whoever records hadith, his proof is strengthened. Whoever learns jurisprudence, his status is ennobled. Whoever learns Arabic, his disposition becomes gentle. Whoever learns mathematics, his opinion will be copious. And whoever fails to defend his honor will not benefit from his knowledge.[134]

This is the end of what Ibn Rajab al-Ḥanbalī related in his treatise, *The Heirs of the Prophets*. And the last of our prayers is, *All praise is for Allah, the Lord of all the worlds.*

NOTES

1. This hadith is related in the following sources: Imām Aḥmad ibn Ḥanbal, *al-Musnad*, (Beirut, Lebanon: al-Maktab al-Islāmī, 1985), 5:196; Abū Dāwūd al-Sajastānī, *al-Sunan* (Beirut: Dār al-Fikr, 1979), hadith no. 3641; Abū ʿĪsā al-Tirmidhī, *al-Jāmiʿ* (Cairo: Dār Iḥyāʾ al-Turāth al-ʿArabī, 1938), hadith no. 2682; Ibn Mājah, *al-Sunan*, ed. Fuʾād ʿAbd al-Bāqī (Beirut: Dār al-Kutub al-ʿIlmiyya, 1987), hadith no. 223; al-Dārimī, *al-Sunan* (Cairo: Dār al-Fikr, 1978), 1:98; Ibn Ḥibbān, *al-Ṣaḥīḥ*, ed. Shuʿayb al-Arnaʾūṭ (Beirut: Muʾassasa al-Risāla, 1984), hadith no. 88; al-Baghawī, *Sharḥ al-Sunna* (Beirut: al-Maktab al-Islāmī, 1983), hadith no. 129; Ibn ʿAbd al-Barr, *Jāmiʿ Bayān al-ʿIlm* (Cairo: Dār al-Kutub al-Islāmiyya, 1982), pp. 63, 68; and al-Khaṭīb al-Baghdādī, *al-Riḥla fi Ṭalab al-Ḥadīth* (Beirut: Dār al-Kutub al-ʿIlmiyya, 1970), pp. 77, 82.
2. Imām al-Bukhārī, *al-Jāmiʿ al-Ṣaḥīḥ* (Beirut: Dār Iḥyāʾ al-Turāth al-ʿArabī, 1990), hadith no. 5002.
3. Al-Dhahabī, *Siyar Aʿlām al-Nubalāʾ* (Beirut: Muʾassasa al-Risāla, 1983), 2:342.
4. Abū Nuʿaym, *Ḥilyatu'l-Awliyāʾ* (Beirut: Dār al-Kitāb al-ʿArabī, 1985), 2:95.
5. Al-Khaṭīb, *al-Faqīh wa'l-Mutafaqqih* (Beirut: Dār al-Kutub al-ʿIlmiyya, 1980), 2:177.
6. Bukhārī, hadith no. 4590.
7. This incident is mentioned by al-Khaṭīb al-Baghdādī in *al-Riḥla*, hadith no. 52; and in *Tafsīr Ibn Kathīr* (his commentary on verse 2:196). This incident is most commonly related from Saʿd ibn Isḥāq,

from Abān, from Ḥasan al-Baṣrī, "I traveled from Baṣra to Kūfā to visit Ka'b ibn 'Ujrah, I asked him, 'What was your atonement when you were afflicted with *al-adhā* [an affliction to the head]?' He replied, "A female sheep.' "

8. Tirmidhī, hadith no. 2650, 2651; and Ibn Mājah, hadith no. 247, 249.
9. Imām Aḥmad, *Kitāb al-Zuhd* (Beirut: Dār al-Kutub al-'Ilmiyya,1983), 2:16; and Abū Nu'aym, *al-Ḥilya*, 1:239.
10. Imām Aḥmad, *Kitāb al-Zuhd*, 2:242.
11. See citations in note 1, above.
12. Imām Muslim, *al-Jāmi' al-Ṣaḥīḥ*, ed. Fu'ād 'Abd al-Bāqī (Cairo: Maṭba'a 'Īsā al-Bābī al-Ḥalabī, 1954), hadith no. 2699.
13. Imām al-Suyūṭī, *al-Durr al-Manthūr* (Beirut: Dār al-Ma'rifa, 1970), 2:135. He references al-Ṭabarī and 'Abd al-Hamīd who quote Qatada.
14. Abū Nu'aym, *al-Ḥilya*. He relates it from Imām Aḥmad, from Yazīd bin Hārūn, from Hāmid al-Ṭawīl, from Anas, from the Prophet ﷺ. It is likely to be a fabricated hadith because Imām Aḥmad doesn't narrate from this particular chain of transmission.
15. Ibn Abī Shayba, *al-Musannaf* (Cairo: Dār al-Furqān), hadith no. 17185; al-Ḥilya, 2:177.
16. Imām Aḥmad, *al-Musnad*, 3:157, and Khaṭīb, *al-Faqīh*, 2:70.
17. Bukhārī, hadith no. 100, 7307.
18. Tirmidhī, hadith no. 2653.
19. Al-Nasā'ī, *al-Sunan al-Kubra* (Beirut: Dār Iḥyā' al-Turāth al-'Arabī), 8:211; *al-Musnad*, 6:26–27; al-Ḥākim, *al-Mustadrak* (Beirut: Dār al-Kutub al-'Ilmiyya, 1990), 1:99–100.
20. Imām Aḥmad, *al-Musnad*, 4:218–19; Ibn Mājah, hadith no. 4048.
21. Related with a similar wording in *al-Ḥilya*, 1:281; *al-Zuhd*, 2:135.
22. Al-Dārimī, 1:102.
23. Muslim, hadith no. 722.
24. Muslim, hadith no. 2722.
25. Ibn Ḥibbān, hadith no. 82. Al-Haythamī mentioned it as well. *Majma' al-Zawā'id* (Beirut: Dār al-Kitāb al-'Arabī, 1967), 10:181–82.
26. Muslim, as part of a larger hadith, hadith no. 223.

27. This meaning is attributed to the Prophet ﷺ. It is related by Ibn Mājah, hadith no. 4049; and al-Ḥākim, 4:473.
28. Abū Nuʿaym, *al-Ḥilya*, 4:54.
29. Al-Dārimī, *al-Sunan*, 1:102; Abū Nuʿaym, *al-Ḥilya*, 7:280.
30. Imām Aḥmad, *al-Zuhd* (Beirut: Dār al-Kutub al-ʿIlmiyya, 1983), 2:106; and Abū Nuʿaym, *al-Ḥilya*, 1:131.
31. ʿAbdallāh ibn al-Mubārak, *Kitāb al-Zuhd* (Beirut: Dār al-Kutub al-ʿIlmiyya, 1983), p. 15; and Imām Aḥmad, *al-Zuhd*, 2:106.
32. Al-Dārimī, 1:102.
33. See al-Dhahabī, *Siyar Aʿlām al-Nubalā'*, 4:229–32, for an account of the tribulation of Saʿīd ibn al-Musayyib. Also see Ibn Jawzī, *Manāqib Imām Aḥmad*, (Beirut: Dār al-Afāq, 1981), p. 342.
34. Al-Ḥajjāj ibn Artah was a scholar known to be obsessed with status and prestige. See al-Dhahabī, *Siyar Aʿlām al-Nubalā'*, 7:72.
35. Abū ʿAbd al-Raḥmān al-Sulamī, *Ṭabaqāt al-Ṣūfiyya*, ed. Nūruddīn al-Shariba (Cairo: Maktaba al-Khafijī, 1986), p. 356. Among the saying of Junayd, "All paths [*ṭuruq*] to Allah are closed to mankind, except to one who treads in the footsteps of the Messenger ﷺ, implements his *sunna*, and adheres to his path. By so doing, [he finds] all the paths leading to good accessible," as quoted in al-Sulamī, *Ṭabaqāt al-Ṣūfiyya*, p. 356.
36. Abū Nuʿaym, *al-Ḥilya*, pp. 79–80.
37. Al-Khaṭīb, *al-Faqīh*, 1:13. Its chain of transmission is broken.
38. Imām Aḥmad, *al-Musnad*, 3:150; and Tirmidhī, hadith no. 3510.
39. Al-Khaṭīb, *al-Faqīh*, 1:13.
40. Al-Khaṭīb, *al-Faqīh*, 1:17.
41. This is a sound hadith which has been related from Anas ibn Mālik, ʿAbdallāh ibn ʿUmar, Abū Saʿīd al-Khudrī, and ʿAbdallāh ibn Masʿūd.
42. Tirmidhī, hadith no. 487.
43. Al-Khaṭīb, *al-Faqīh*, 1:45. Its chain of transmission is weak.
44. Al-Khaṭīb, *al-Faqīh*, 1:45.
45. Al-Khaṭīb, *al-Faqīh*, 1:45.
46. Al-Khaṭīb, *al-Faqīh*, 2:167.

47. Al-Khaṭīb, *al-Faqīh*, 2:167.
48. Al-Khaṭīb, *al-Faqīh*, 2:167.
49. Ibn ʿAbd al-Barr, p. 89.
50. Al-Khaṭīb, *al-Faqīh*, 2:161; and al-Ājurī, *Akhlāq al-ʿUlamā'* (Cairo: Dār al-Miṣriyya, 1991), pp. 49–50.
51. Ibn Mājah, hadith no. 226; *al-Musnad*, 4:239–41.
52. Al-Khaṭīb, *al-Riḥla*, pp. 85–86.
53. Ibn Qayyim al-Jawziyya, *Miftāḥ al-Saʿāda* (Beirut: Dār al-Kutub al-ʿIlmiyya, 1970), 1:64.
54. Al-Ājurī, p. 20.
55. Tirmidhī, hadith no. 2685. He declared it a sound hadith.
56. Both al-Haythamī and al-ʿIrāqī reject al-Azdī's criticism of one of this hadith's narrators, Ismāʿīl ibn Zarara. They both affirm his soundness.
57. Ibn Najjār al-Hindī, *Kanz al-ʿUmmāl* (Aleppo, Syria: Maktaba al-Turāth al-Islāmī, 1983), hadith no. 28679.
58. Imām Aḥmad, *al-Musnad*, 5:6.
59. Al-Ḥākim, 2:418.
60. Ibn ʿAbbās relates that when a believer passes away the place of his prostrations on Earth weeps for him, as does the gate in Heaven though which his good deeds ascend. They don't weep for a nonbeliever. See *Tafsīr Ibn Kathīr* on this verse.
61. See *Tafsīr Ibn Jarīr al-Ṭabarī* (Cairo: Dār al-Maʿārif, 1957), 3:249.
62. Bukhārī, hadith no. 118, 2350.
63. Ibn Mājah, hadith no. 4021.
64. See *Tafsīr al-Ṭabarī*, 3:255–56.
65. Ibn ʿAbd al-Barr, p. 30.
66. This was said by ʿUmar bin ʿAbd al-ʿAzīz, as related by Ibn Abī Khaythama, *al-ʿIlm* (Beirut: al-Maktab al-Islāmī), p. 110.
67. Ibn Rajab, *Dhayl Ṭabaqāt al-Ḥanābila*, 1:431.
68. Abū Nuʿaym, *al-Ḥilya*, 4:273; Ibn Saʿd, *al-Ṭabaqāt* (Beirut: Dār al-Ṣadr), 6:257.
69. See *Tafsīr al-Ṭabarī* on this verse.
70. Bukhārī, hadith no. 3327; Muslim, hadith no. 2834.

71. See al-Suyūṭī, 6:185.
72. Tirmidhī, hadith no. 2681; Ibn Mājah, hadith no. 222.
73. Ibn Mājah, hadith no. 229.
74. Ibn Mubārak, p. 488.
75. Al-Khaṭīb, *al-Faqīh*, 1:15.
76. Al-Haythamī, *Kashf al-Astār* (Beirut: Mu'assasa al-Risāla), hadith no. 139; al-Ḥākim, *al-Mustadrak*, 1:92–93; Abū Nuʿaym, 2:211–12.
77. Al-Mundharī, *al-Targhīb wa'l-Tarhīb* (Cairo: Dār al-Ḥadīth, 1989), 1:60.
78. Ibn Mājah, hadith no. 219.
79. Al-Khaṭīb, *al-Faqīh*, 1:16.
80. Ibn ʿAbd al-Barr, p. 50.
81. Al-Khaṭīb, *al-Faqīh*, 1:16.
82. Al-Dārimī, 1:82.
83. Al-Dhahabī, 1:493.
84. Al-Khaṭīb, *al-Faqīh*, 1:16.
85. Ibn Abī Shayba, hadith no. 17050.
86. Abū Nuʿaym, *al-Ḥilya*, 6:366.
87. Abū Nuʿaym, *al-Ḥilya*, 9:119.
88. Ibn ʿAbd al-Barr, p. 15.
89. Al-Khaṭīb, *al-Faqīh*, 1:17.
90. Ibn ʿAbd al-Barr, p. 50; al-Khaṭīb, *Sharaf Aṣḥāb al-Ḥadīth* (Ankara, Turkey: Ankara University, 1971), p. 84.
91. Al-Khaṭīb, *Tārīkh Baghdād* (Beirut: Dār al-Kitāb al-ʿArabī, 1975), 2:193. It is said to be a fabricated hadith.
92. Tirmidhī, hadith no. 2647.
93. Al-Haythamī, *Kashf al-Astār*, p. 138.
94. Abū Nuʿaym, *al-Ḥilya*, 1:239.
95. Al-Khaṭīb, *al-Faqīh*, 1:15–16.
96. See *Tafsīr al-Ṭabarī* on this verse.
97. Bukhārī, hadith no. 20.
98. Ibn Wāsiʿ is reputed to have said, "If sins had a foul odor, no one

would have sat with me." His biography is mentioned by Abū Nuʿaym, *al-Ḥilya*, 2:345–57.

99. Ibn al-Jawzī, *al-Quṣṣāṣ wa'l-Mudhakkirīn* (Beirut: Dār al-Kutub al-ʿIlmiyya, 1986), hadith no. 140.

100. Tirmidhī, 5:50. This saying is attributed to Fuḍayl ibn ʿIyāḍ.

101. Among the sayings of the righteous forbears on this issue is that of ʿUmar ibn ʿAbd al-ʿAzīz, "One who acts without knowledge corrupts more than he rectifies." Related by Ibn ʿAbd al-Barr, p. 54; and al-Khaṭīb, *al-Faqīh*, 1:19.

102. Qāḍī ʿIyāḍ, *al-Ilmāʿ* (Beirut: al-Maktab al-Islāmī, 1983), p. 17; Abū Nuʿaym, *Akhbār Iṣfahān*, Leiden, Holland: Brill, 1924), 1:80. It is said to be a fabricated hadith.

103. Abū Nuʿaym, *al-Ḥilya*, 3:153.

104. Al-Khaṭīb, *al-Faqīh*, 1:35.

105. Al-Khaṭīb, *al-Faqīh*, 1:35.

106. Abū Nuʿaym, *al-Ḥilya*, 8:254.

107. Ibn Mājah, hadith no. 4313.

108. Al-Khaṭīb, *al-Faqīh*, 1:20.

109. Al-Khaṭīb, *al-Faqīh*, 1:35.

110. Al-Khaṭīb, *Sharaf Aṣḥāb al-Ḥadīth*, p. 50. The term *abdāl* refers to an elite population of Allah's righteous servants who are present among every generation. They are a source of good and blessing for people. Whenever one dies, Allah sends another to replace him. This concept, as testified to by Imām Aḥmad's utterance and by Ibn Rajab's citation, is accepted by the overwhelming majority of the scholars of *Ahl al-Sunna*. The term is similarly mentioned by Ibn Taymiyya in *al-ʿAqīda al-Wasiṭiyya*.

111. Al-Haythamī reports in *Majmaʿ al-Zawā'id*, 1:124, that its chain of transmission is good.

112. Bukhārī, hadith no. 5019.

113. Bukhārī, hadith no. 5022.

114. Muslim, hadith no. 2408.

115. Imām Aḥmad, *al-Musnad*, 2:172, 211.

116. Bukhārī, hadith no. 3096; Muslim, hadith no. 1760.

117. Bukhārī, hadith no. 3098.

118. Abū Nuʿaym, *al-Ḥilya*, 2:131.
119. Tirmidhī, hadith no. 2377; al-Ḥākim, 4:310; and Imām Aḥmad, *al-Musnad*, 1:391, 441.
120. Ibn Ḥibbān, hadith no. 255.
121. Muslim, hadith no. 1631.
122. Abū Nuʿaym, *al-Ḥilya*, 2:373.
123. Abū Nuʿaym, *al-Ḥilya*, 8:93.
124. Abū Nuʿaym, *al-Ḥilya*, 2:158.
125. Abū Nuʿaym, *al-Ḥilya*, 2:147.
126. Al-Dhahabī, 7:270.
127. Ibn al-Jawzī, *Manāqib al-Imām Aḥmad* (Beirut: Dār al-Afāq, 1981), pp. 250–54.
128. Abū Nuʿaym, *al-Ḥilya*, 9:241.
129. Al-Dhahabī, 7:127.
130. Ibn al-Jawzī, *Ṣayd al-Khāṭir* (Beirut: Dār al-Kutub al-ʿIlmiyya, 1985), p. 210.
131. Abū Nuʿaym, *al-Ḥilya*, 4:136.
132. Ibn Mājah, hadith no. 257; Abū Nuʿaym, 2:105.
133. Abū Nuʿaym, *al-Ḥilya*, 2:150–51.
134. Al-Khaṭīb, *Sharaf Aṣḥāb al-Ḥadīth*, p. 69.

QURANIC VERSE INDEX

SUBJECT INDEX